About the author

Gennady Levitsky immigrated to the USA from the Soviet Union in 1983 at the age of thirty-two. For thirty-three years he worked as an electrical engineer for different companies. He retired in 2017. Facing the prospect of becoming a couch potato and annoyance to the members of his household he decided to concentrate on writing his recollections and sharing them with anyone willing to learn more about life in the unique historical phenomenon called the Soviet Union.

This is a work of fiction. Names, characters, businesses, places, events and incidents are either the products of the author's imagination or used in a fictitious manner. Any resemblance to actual persons, living or dead, or actual events is purely coincidental.

THE LEPERS

Gennady Levitsky

THE LEPERS

Vanguard Press

VANGUARD PAPERBACK

© Copyright 2023
Gennady Levitsky

The right of Gennady Levitsky to be identified as author of this work has been asserted by him in accordance with the Copyright, Designs and Patents Act 1988.

All Rights Reserved

No reproduction, copy or transmission of this publication may be made without written permission.
No paragraph of this publication may be reproduced, copied or transmitted save with the written permission of the publisher, or in accordance with the provisions of the Copyright Act 1956 (as amended).

Any person who commits any unauthorised act in relation to this publication may be liable to criminal prosecution and civil claims for damages.

A CIP catalogue record for this title is available from the British Library.

ISBN 978 1 80016 615 8

*Vanguard Press is an imprint of
Pegasus Elliot Mackenzie Publishers Ltd.*
www.pegasuspublishers.com

First Published in 2023

**Vanguard Press
Sheraton House Castle Park
Cambridge England**

Printed & Bound in Great Britain

Dedication

To the "prisoners of Zion", Soviet "refuseniks" and dissidents. Their heroic acts and sacrifices breached the Soviet wall and allowed thousands of oppressed and humiliated people to find their way to freedom.

Acknowledgements

I would like to thank the editor, Paul Kelly, for his part in bringing this book to a reader-friendly form.

Prologue

Before you start to read my memoirs, I would like to explain the reason I decided to write them.

First of all, I think, a short introduction into the scope of my recollections might benefit both of us: you, as a reader and me, as a writer. You, in the sense, that you won't need to read several pages before realizing that you are wasting your time; and me — because it gives me an opportunity to apologize for grammatical omissions and unconventionally structured sentences which you may encounter in my narrative: in no way I had an intention to introduce into English language stylistic innovations or novel expressions; they are just the consequence of my multilingual limitations (English is not my first language and I learned it quite late).

Now let me tell you how it all started.

A couple of weeks ago, just before the Jewish holiday of Rosh Hashanah, my daughter approached me with a strange question:

"Daddy, did you come to America illegally?"

"What? Of course not," I said, slightly surprised by her inquiry: "Why did you ask me? You were never interested in this part of my biography."

"Well," she said, "yesterday in school we had a discussion in our sociology class about illegal immigrants and about the problems they are facing during their integration into American society, and everybody got very excited when I told them that my dad, most likely, also came to America from Russia illegally…"

"Wait a second. Who told you that? First of all, I didn't come from Russia. I came from Lithuania. And secondly, definitely not illegally."

"Not illegally? How pitiful! And you just said — from Lithuania? I always thought you came from Russia. Is Lithuania a different country?"

"Right now — yes, it is. Right now Lithuania is an independent state but when I left, it was part of the Soviet Union together with other fourteen republics."

"What do you mean by fourteen other republics? What republics? What are you talking about? Do you mean that Russia consists of different republics just like we here, in USA, have different states?"

"Well, again, not exactly. Russia was just one of the fifteen republics. Together they formed the Soviet Union. On one hand there were more differences between various Soviet republics than there are between states in the USA, but on the other hand — less. Each one of them was controlled by the central government in Moscow. This government implanted trusted people into every sphere and institution of each of fifteen republics. Take, for example, the Soviet secret police, the KGB…"

"Oh, yeah, KGB! I have heard a lot about it. In the movies. Was this organization indeed as brutal as movies portray it? Did it put millions of innocent people into concentration camps?"

"Look, it was a little bit more complicated than you see in the movies. I cannot explain everything in just two words. Besides there were different times also. The reign of Stalin, for example, was quite different from the Brezhnev era. In the 1930s KGB agents (it was called NKVD then) indeed, under the cover of the night, were coming to arrest people, to deport them and often without any trial. But during my time the KGB didn't act that way."

"Very interesting. And how about you, dad? Did the KGB ever arrest you or you were too young to be arrested?"

Her questions were coming at me one after another like snowflakes from the winter skies. Finally I had to give up.

"Listen," I said to her, "Why don't you write down all your questions and I will look through them and answer to the best of my ability."

However, when two hours later she handed me several pages of the printed text, I realized that my task would be a little bit more complicated than I initially assumed. She was interested in everything starting from the conditions of my apartment in Lithuania to the Holocaust, to the fate of the Jewish community in our city and especially she was fascinated by the KGB and its influence on our everyday life. Basically — she was interested in everything."

"I discussed with my friends whatever you have told me this morning," she said, "and they were very disappointed that you were not an illegal immigrant. Nevertheless we worked out a few questions for you and are anxious to hear your answers."

"How could I possibly answer so many questions?" I asked her, puzzled.

"This is not a problem, dad. You could write your answers on a paper, just like I did," she suggested compassionately, "and me and my friends, can look at your notes later, at our convenience."

(She, as well as her peers, is constantly busy, either in school or on the cell phone).

The questions were not in a systematic order, but chaotic, without any obvious link or correlation between them. Therefore the first thing I decided to do was to rearrange their sequence, to combine similar questions into specific groups, according to the subject, topic and time of reference and then to answer them, if possible, collectively.

It was during this process when I realized the underlying nature of this enterprise: in all my answers the description of the Soviet reality could be presented only through the eyes of my own personal experience.

This discovery compelled me to look at the project from a different angle. If you think about it — I was a witness of a peculiar culture, a part of the unusual society which some other countries tried to duplicate but never succeeded and unlikely will ever do. It means that many details of this major social experiment of the twentieth century could be lost forever, particularly the ones which dealt with the human relations and interactions. At the same time, I presume, there are and certainly will be curious individuals, apart from my daughter and her friends, who may become interested in how people lived in the Soviet Union and what caused its sudden collapse and disintegration. While I don't pretend to have a comprehensive answer to this tricky question, particularly since as a Jew I may have a somewhat skewed view on the subject, further aggravated by the fact that I lived in Lithuania and not in Russia, nevertheless, my knowledge and insights may still help future history geeks to uncover the correct picture. I say this because I belong to a small group of individuals who not only shared the same kind of experience but who also have the means to communicate it to the representatives of a different cultural background without meddling by unscrupulous censors, pressure from editors and deficiencies of the translations, which, in my view, could be attributed to the lack of the familiarity with the translated material. My work thus might give a chance to an unfamiliar reader to look at the Soviet society through the eyes of one of the participants, instead of relying on some "secret archives", limited experience of the outsiders or on fictional material, like Orwell's book *Animal Farm*. In other words: by answering these kinds of questions I can accomplish much more than just answering them.

From such theoretical observations to the idea of writing memoirs, as you can imagine, was just one little step.

"I think you have a very good point," agreed my wife when I shared my ambitious plan with her. "Such activity should be quite beneficial for your mental and overall health. Do it for sure. I agree. But first you need to finish the guest room in our basement, the one you started a couple years ago, rake the leaves in our yard and finally clean up your wardrobe closet you have been promising me in the last three days."

So, I had to move into the basement, together with my laptop computer, to contemplate the possible ways of accomplishing this challenging task.

Prior to this mission I had no clue how it might be difficult even to start it; let alone to deal with many subsequent obstacles and pitfalls . Shall I begin my recollections from the day I was born? I guess that is what other people usually do when they write their biographies. But who am I to make anyone interested in my childhood or my adolescence? Am I a world celebrity? A football star?

No, this is not the right way to do it. I should find in my past an event or some incident which changed my life in some important or unexpected way, and at the same time, be related to the original objective: to provide comprehensive and truthful answers to the tricky questions of my daughter and her classmates.

While I was sitting in the basement staring at the blank display of the computer and considering how to start my notes and what my first sentence should look like, a tiny ray of autumn sun peeped through the dusty basement's window, penetrated the tangled mosaic of the spiderweb and lay on my lap, soft and warm like a kitten. The arrival of this unexpected guest prompted me to look at our backyard, at the red and yellow leaves scampering over the withered lawn and the picture of another fall in another country suddenly emerged from the inner depths of my memory. Indeed, how many years have passed from the moment when we decided to leave the place we grew up and move to a strange land many thousands of miles away?

Consequently, I remembered all the other details of our voyage: our sojourners, the refugees who travelled with us, young and old, cautious, and brave, motivated, and accidental; I remembered their fears and their hopes and the tears in the eyes of our relatives, the ones we were leaving behind, and the luring temptation of the universe that was waiting for us ahead. And of course, I remembered my old and dear friends.

And then I thought — okay, but wouldn't someone be interested to find out "why did we do it?"

What triggered in our minds such a radical idea? Was life in the Soviet Union indeed so unbearable that we had no other choice but to leave? We were not fleeing a war or genocide as most other refugees did.

I looked at the questions I promised to answer and to my sheer surprise I found among them very similar ones. And the decision of how, from which year, to start my memoirs came on its own, abruptly and effortlessly: all I needed to do was to provide a reliable description of those bygone days — the days of our discontent, awaiting and departure that we all, "Russian" immigrants, went through, and to tell the readers about the people I met on my way to a free world and hope that my limited abilities as a narrator won't unduly diminish their stories because their stories themselves are the answers to most of the questions.

So, after a short deliberation, I came to the conclusion that I will commence my notes from one specific day, the last day of the Indian summer, the day I and my friends for the first time came together to attend the service in Kaunas synagogue. Why? Well, first, because coincidentally, today is the anniversary of that day, if you count years according to the Hebrew calendar, and second... well, because the season of autumn has a special meaning to Jews.

Mikhail Rothman

Yes, the season of autumn has a special meaning to Jews: it is the time of the Jewish holidays, a time of joyful celebrations and remorseful prayers, spiritual meditations and exciting rituals, a time of recollection, assessments, and divine judgment.

In Lithuania it is also a rainy time: day after day and night after night the rain patters on the cobblestone streets and on the tin roofs of the old medieval buildings, forms impassable puddles and strips deciduous trees from their beautiful garments. It is cold and gloomy and inhospitable outside as if nature itself mourns over the departed summer setting everyone's mood into the state of the muffled melancholy and nostalgia.

But within this stretch of the dismal weather there is a short period of time when the rain takes a break and the clouds move apart, revealing pristine blue skies and then a sun, in the gracious gesture of farewell, would ignite the soggy Baltic landscape in the magnificent colors of decaying foliage.

In the evening of one of such summer-like days, at the advent of Yom Kippur — the holiest day of the Jewish calendar — in the tiny courtyard of the Kaunas choral synagogue a group of elderly Jews passionately debate the latest world news. The sun is almost gone; just its last slanted rays still continue to adorn the fallen leaves and the rusted fence, several naked trees along it, and the peeling walls of the formerly impressive but now slowly decaying edifice.

Built in the second half of the nineteenth century at the confluence of the two busy streets, Savanoryu and Ozeskenes, it stands as a sorrowful reminder of those old but not too distant days when the third of the city's population spoke Yiddish and when this building was just one of many houses of prayer. The majority of the Jewish residents lived then on the opposite side of the Neris river, in the impoverished neighborhood by the name "Slobodka", the home of the famous "Slobodka yeshiva" and later, during Nazi occupation, the site of the Jewish ghetto. Nazis choose it not by accident: at the turn of the twentieth century it was swarming with the poor Jewish folk — from the owners of the petty shops to their penniless customers, from skillful shoemakers to gifted musicians, from scholars and famous rabbis to their disciples and students. Only if someone could become rich enough to cross the river and settle in the more prestigious and predominantly Gentile neighborhood, only then he or she had the opportunity to say a holiday prayer in a place like this.

Times have changed. Today, with only a handful of the Jewish residents and even fewer congregants this house of prayers can accommodate everyone, wishing to repent his or her sins on such a special occasion.

The sun is almost gone, but no one hurries inside. Among all the qualities possessed by the members of the Jewish community the notion of punctuality is an alien one, a sort of unnecessary intricacy which might complicate their already hectic lives. Who needs these additional obligations? After all, they have more than twenty-four hours to repent their sins: what difference could a few extra minutes make?

We, the youngsters, don't want to be associated with this crowd of the eagerly gesturing folks — the last survivors of the vanishing Yiddish-speaking world. We are people of the new generation, more cultured and more educated, and therefore we are staying away from them on the autumn gilded pathway, which leads from the street to the entrance of the synagogue, encircling our mentor and teacher of Hebrew, Mikhail Rothman. And although he may look just as old as those spirited folks in the courtyard, in reality, he is only few years older than we are and his misleading appearance is probably due to his thick, prematurely turning gray beard or, perhaps, to the astute gaze in his eyes — the witnesses of the hardships that brought on him his Zionist activities: the expulsion from the prestigious Moscow university, lengthy detentions in police stations, psychiatric wards, charges of "petty hooliganism"... At one point even his own parents officially disowned him.

They both worked in public schools: the mother as a teacher and the father as a principal. One day they were summoned to the local KGB office and the head of the "Jewish section" Major Sidorhuck told them: "How could you inoculate your students to the notions of social justice and brotherhood if you couldn't educate your own son? How could you teach them to be patriots of our country if your own son is a disloyal Zionist and fascist?"

And Mikhail's parents agreed with him: indeed, it looked like professional incompetence. They had to make a choice between their son and their job. And they choose the job.

An orphan with still living parents is not a common phenomenon in our society. But who are we going to blame for that? Shall we blame Major Sidorchuk? No, of course not. He did what he had to do, and he is not a bad man, after all. I know him quite well — he is one of our neighbors and lives across the street in the pompous building which was built several years ago for the KGB employees and their families. Nobody is supposed to know his position in that scary organization, but everyone does. Each time he meets my parents on the street he complains to them: "Do you know that your son got into bad company? Are you aware that he attends illegal Hebrew language classes? You'd better take care of this now, before it might become too late and he will end like that disgusting bastard Rothman, his Hebrew teacher. Our labour camps have missed him, I can tell you. He and his buddies Zionists make too many problems for us. Not a single day passes without their mischief. I have a bad feeling that their actions will cause me to die prematurely from a heart attack. I can confess to you (since you are my neighbors) and tell that at this moment of my life I have only one dream, only one desire — it is to see all of you, Jews, boarding airplanes to fly from here into your cursed state of Israel."

Unfortunately for Major Sidorchuk his dream didn't materialize, and he had died from a heart attack just several months before the start of the mass Jewish immigration to Israel. The locals, who knew everything, testified that his last words were: "Those bloody Jewish Zionists..."

"Those bloody Jewish Zionists..." I don't know about Mikhail's friends but Mikhail himself became a devoted Zionist at the age of seven, when he visited the apartment of his classmate Abram Frenkel and noticed on the kitchen table a colorful postcard depicting a tanned muscular man on the orange tractor and some kind of exotic tropical vegetation in the background.

"What is this?" he asked his friend pointing at the postcard.

"This is a kibbutz in Israel," said Abram, "The postcard came from our relatives who live there."

Kibbutz and Israel. These were two new words Mikhail had never heard of before.

"Kibbutz," explained Abram, "is a collective farm just like our kolkhoz and Israel is a Jewish country."

Jewish country? Mikhail never suspected Jews have their own country. As a matter of fact, a day or two earlier he was contemplating how it is unfair for the Jews not to have one. Indeed, he thought, Lithuanians have it, and Russians have it, and even Scots have the place they call Scotland, and only we, Jews, don't have it.

"Why?" he had asked himself. "Why do we need to call a "home" someone else's territory — a place where we are not welcome and constantly mistreated? Why can't we have our own? Are we guilty of something and therefore don't deserve it?"

But here he came with the discovery: he was wrong — Jews have their own country; just not every Jew has the right to live in it.

The rays of the fading sun had already left the rooftop of the synagogue and climbed up towards the heavens and colored a distant solitary cloud in different shades of pink and gray. The sharpness of the daylight had slowly melted into the chilly evening air. Just as a calm comes before the storm, so the skies turned pale and shallow before they fell into the darkness, before they could reveal to the world the first star; the star which would announce the start of the new day, the Day of Atonement, the fearsome Day of

Judgment.

"It comes on the tenth day after Jewish New Year, Rosh Hashanah," Mikhail tells us lighting up his next cigarette. "On that day God examines each person's deeds and decides his or her fate for the future. In order to repent their sins Jews must pray all day long and fast. But after Yom Kippur we have a joyful holiday of Sukkoth. The last day of Sukkoth has a special name. It is called Simhas Toire. This is the only day of the Jewish calendar when women and men could pray together in one room."

"Why do they have to pray separately on all other days?" asks Maya Katz.

Maya Katz is the only girl in our group. Soon she will leave us and go upstairs to join other women in the upper gallery of the synagogue.

"Having separate areas for men and women has nothing to do with the discrimination," explains Mikhail. "The purpose of this tradition is to prevent males from looking at the women during time of prayers, so that women's beauty and sexual appeal could not distract them from the holy matters."

I am not convinced that this is the reason. At least regarding Maya Katz since her sexual appeal could hardly distract anybody from anything. She is one of the ugliest girls I have ever met. And an unlucky one too. I know for a fact that she joined our group not because of her interest in Hebrew language or in Jewish history but because she is crazy about our teacher Mikhail Rothman. Unfortunately for her, he already has a beautiful Gentile wife, a stunning "shikse" by the name Laima, the object of our common envy and admiration. How could this swarthy and lopsided Jewish girl compete with the dazzling qualities of her rival? What might she offer in exchange? The only asset Maya has is her uncle living now in Israel because having such close relatives outside USSR is the necessary condition to obtain emigration permit, but it won't be enough to lure Mikhail. After all, there are other Jewesses with the similar kind of assets.

Actually Mikhail won't need them anyway for in the years to come Soviet authorities, fed up with his mischievous activities of "petty hooliganism", will issue him with the exit visa without the usual bureaucratic formalities and on one special day he finally will leave the country of his birth and will move to the country of his dream. In this new country, in Israel, he will be greeted like a hero, with the fanfare and accolade, and will spend the first few weeks meeting the Israeli president, celebrities and members of the Knesset. And then everybody will forget about him. Without proper education and practical skills, he won't be able to find a decent job and will end up in his previous vocation as a cashier in some godforsaken little grocery store in the similarly forsaken little town of Afula. His beautiful Lithuanian wife, "the shikse" Laima, who so much admired him back in Lithuania, will leave him for an old and wealthy Moroccan Jew. But nothing will break his spirit; nothing will make him change his views. On the barren hills of Judean desert and on the dreary mounds of Samaria he will raise Israel flags and build primitive huts, claiming Jewish sovereignty over this ancient land in defiance of the "international law" and Israeli left-wing politicians, and harassing Israeli security service Shin Bet the way he previously harassed KGB.

A short historical journey

I decided to include this brief narrative regarding Jewish impact on the history of Lithuania because without it the readers might have difficulty in understanding some of the actions and motives of the people I intend to mention in my notes.

Thus… let me start.

The first documented evidence of the Jewish presence on the Lithuanian soil is a decree issued by the Lithuanian king Vytautas the Great on June 24, 1388. It granted the Jews of the town of Trakai certain rights and privileges.

I will skip another 600 years of the mutual coexistence and refer anybody interested in this part of the history to the books and articles readily available in libraries or on the internet. Because, for all its richness and obvious importance to the history geeks, this period of time had little impact on my life and on the lives of my friends and relatives. I noticed only one peculiarity: for all this time Christians and Jews lived separately, apart from each other, with the minimal interaction between two communities. Their substantial intermingling started only at the beginning of the twentieth century.

I will begin, therefore, from the year 1918, when by the end of World War One, Lithuania, after hundreds of years of subservient existence, regained its full national independence. The rebirth didn't happen peacefully: right from the start Lithuania got involved in a bloody war with Poland over its ancient capital, the city of Vilnius, designated by the leaders of the newly born nation to its previous role. However, six hundred years made a significant change in the demographic makeup of the city. By 1918 almost half of the population were Poles and at least one third Jews. Ethnical Lithuanians represented just a tiny minority. The government of Poland considered the city to be a Polish property.

The Poles won the war and incorporated the entire Vilnius district with its one hundred thousand Jewish residents into their territory. Disheartened Lithuanians declared by its size the second city of Kaunas to be their "temporary' or "provisional" capital.

To compensate themselves for the loss of Vilnius Lithuanians in 1923 captured the major port on the Baltic Sea, the city of Memel and renamed it Klaipeda. (Under the Treaty of Versailles Memel Territory was detached from Germany and made a protectorate of the Entente while the French became provisional administrators of the region until a more permanent solution could be worked out.)

Until 1926 Lithuania was a democratic republic. But in December of that year the legitimate government was overthrown by the military coup. The leaders of the coup deposed president Grinius and replaced him with the chief of the Nationalist party Antanas Smetona, who later became the "president for life".

Despite the dictatorial essence of the new government, the living conditions for common folks in the years between two wars were quite good: the country experienced cultural renaissance and an unprecedented economic growth. It particularly benefited local Jews, who after hundreds of years of depravity and persecution finally achieved equal status and became full-fledged citizens. Never before had they had such an opportunity to express themselves in different fields of social life. Yeshivas, synagogues, cultural and sport clubs, youth organizations, theaters, press and businesses — all of these began to flourish in the post-World War One era. For example, although Jews comprised less than ten percent of the population, they owned more than half of the country's factories and small businesses, dominated in commerce and the financial sphere and represented the majority of lawyers and doctors. The only doors which remained closed to them were the doors to the chambers of power: you wouldn't find a single Jew among high-ranking military officers, among chiefs of police or Smetona's close cronies. Apparently, due to such unfairness, many of the Lithuanian Jews still felt discriminated and disenfranchised. Quite likely that was the reason why such feelings led them to join the illegal, at that time, Lithuanian communist party.

There is a lot of controversy regarding Jewish participation in this clandestine organization. The majority of Lithuanians perceived it as, if not totally, then overwhelmingly, a "party of Jews". But this was not true. The Communist party of Lithuania during the reign of Smetona never exceeded several hundred members, half of whom probably indeed were Jews. However three or even four hundred people out of a hundred and fifty thousand Jews was not more than just a drop of water in the ocean.

The clear skies over Lithuania began to cloud in 1933 when the Nazis gained power in Germany. They put a lot of pressure on the Lithuanian government demanding the return of the city of Memel. The intensity of this demand grew steadily over the years and in March of 1939 (just five days after the invasion in Czechoslovakia) Germany finally issued the ultimatum: "Give Memel to Germany or face full scale invasion". The signatories of the 1924 convention, which guaranteed protection of the status quo, France and Great Britain, followed their earlier established policy of appeasement and didn't move a finger. On March 24, 1939, Memel became part of Germany.

In August of the same year Germany and the Soviet Union signed an agreement, the so called "Molotov — Ribbentrop pact". The pact had a "secret protocol" which assigned Lithuania to the Soviet "sphere of influence".

On September 1, 1939 the Nazis attacked Poland and started World War Two. Two weeks later the Red Army also moved into Polish territory and occupied its most eastern provinces, including the district of Vilnius. In October the USSR offered it to Lithuania. And the Lithuanian government, after long and heated deliberation, accepted the offer.

However, there is nothing free in this world. Together with the city of Vilnius Lithuania also received Red Army units which were stationed in the district after the invasion. In June of the following year these units moved deeper into Lithuanian territory and took control of the entire country. The Lithuanian military didn't offer any resistance while President Smetona, fearing for his life, fled abroad, landing eventually on American shores.

Beside elements of the Red Army Lithuania also acquired about one hundred thousand Jewish residents living in the Vilnius district and thus the Jewish population of the republic grew approximately to two hundred and fifty thousand and represented now more than ten percent of all citizens.

After taking full control of the country, Soviet bosses announced unscheduled national elections. Only communists and independent candidates were allowed to be chosen.

Despite such severe restrictions many prominent Lithuanian personalities, such as former minister

Venclova, writers Salomeya Neris and Cvirka, and many others were elected in a new parliament. (It was called "Liaudes Seimas"). A well-known left-leaning journalist Justas Paleckis became the new Lithuanian president.

On July 21, 1940 this newly elected Lithuanian government sent the petition to the Supreme Soviet asking for permission to join the "brotherhood of the Soviet nations". On August 3 such permission was magnanimously granted, and it marked the end of Lithuanian independence.

Immediately after staged celebrations, the Soviet secret police (NKVD) moved into the country and started to round up ex-capitalists, nationalists, former chiefs of police, "religious clerics" and other "enemies of the people". The chains of wooden boxcars loaded with the elderly, children and the disabled began to move east, toward uninhabited Siberian wilderness.

But to accomplish their task these NKVD investigators desperately needed help from the local collaborators because without the knowledge of the national specifics, language and recent history, it was very difficult for them to uncover disguised adversaries. The Soviet authorities didn't care about a person's ethnicity or religious background; they only cared about his willingness to support and promote the new regime. No wonder that under such circumstances a lot of Jews (although with a significant amount of the native Lithuanians as well) enthusiastically answered the call of their new masters. Every little shrimp, yearning for power during Smetona's time, could now fulfill his or her dream. Perverts, sycophants, sadists and fervent revolutionaries, eager to repair the world, lined up to become number two in the local hierarchy of bosses. (number one usually was assigned to someone from Russia).

Understandably, the Gentile population saw only Jewish collaborators. The train of thoughts ran like this:

Only a few Lithuanians could work for such a disgusting organization as NKVD because you needed to be a real scumbag to betray your own fatherland. And obviously, there are only a few real scumbags among the largely decent general population. However, for Jews, the situation was different. They don't have a fatherland; Lithuania is not their country. Therefore they don't need to be scumbags to become Russian lackeys. Instead, they would be satisfied with a little bit of power, the quality they had been missing for the last two thousand years.

It didn't make any difference that in reality less than half of NKVD operatives were actually Jewish. Relative to the general proportion of Jews to the rest of population as one to ten, such a situation nevertheless created an impression of the Jewish dominance in that infamous organization.

This circumstance was cleverly used by the Nazi propaganda: it molded in the minds of the local

Gentiles an image of the NKVD tormentor with a big Semitic nose and rapacious eyes. In short, for the vast majority of ethnic Lithuanians the notions of the Bolshevik commissar, NKVD interrogator and a Jew soon became indistinguishable.

Meanwhile Lithuanian patriots did not sit idly. In the fall of 1940 the former Lithuanian ambassador in Germany Kazis Shkirpa (who refused to return after the Red Army occupied his country) with the help of the Nazi military intelligence "Abwehr" founded a Lithuanian anti-communist organization called "The Front of the Lithuanian Activists". Its purpose was to prepare the anti-Soviet revolt as soon as the German army invaded the Soviet Union. Shkirpa was able to establish on Lithuanian territory several secret cells and start preparation for the upcoming uprising. However, in May of 1941 NKVD operatives caught several of his messengers and during interrogations obtained the lists of the co-conspirators.

Therefore, at the beginning of June, the NKVD began to carry out a new wave of mass arrests and deportations. It seized not just real plotters but also suspected, although sometimes innocent people. Usually these were the members of the families of those conspirators or their friends because the NKVD considered everybody who had the knowledge about the plot but didn't report it to the authorities as the enemy's accomplices. According to the various estimates around forty thousand Lithuanians were rounded up at that time and sent on the freight trains to Siberia.

These NKVD efforts, though, were only marginally successful. In less than three weeks the German army attacked the Soviet Union and all remaining members of the "Lithuanian front" staged the long-awaited revolt.

On the day of the German invasion, June 22, 1941 the leadership of the Lithuanian uprising broadcasted on the radio the following statement (partial text):

"Lithuanian brothers and sisters, soon the hour we have been waiting for will come and the Lithuanian nation will get back its national freedom and restore the independence of the state of Lithuania.

Today we rise for a battle against a two-faced enemy. This enemy is the Red Army and Russian Bolshevism...

...The greatest and the most hidden supporter of our enemy is the Jew. He belongs to no nation, to no community. He has neither a homeland nor a country. He is eternally and exclusively a Jew, a servant to the Russian Bolsheviks. He and Russian communists are the one and the same enemy. The ejection of the Russian Bolshevik occupation and the slavery of Jewry is our holy duty and responsibility...

...Vytautas the Great granted Jews the right of refuge in Lithuania, believing they would not transgress the obligations of being polite guests. Jews, however, saw it as an opportunity to exploit — the

bloodsucking tick of Israel insinuating itself into the body of the Lithuanian nation. Speedily they began to spread widely as hustlers, usurers, percentage-gougers, and builders of taverns...

...The evilest NKVD men, informants against Lithuanians and torturers of arrested Lithuanians were and are Jews...

...Jews are exploiters and insatiable bloodsucking parasites of Lithuanian workers, and farmers and urbanites.

The Lithuanian Activist Front in the name of the entire Lithuanian nation solemnly declares:

The ancient right of refuge provided to the Jews during the time of Vytautas the Great is completely and finally rescinded.

Every Jew of Lithuania without exception is hereby officially given notice to leave the land of Lithuania immediately.

Those Jews who have distinguished themselves through betrayal of the Lithuanian state or acts of persecution, torture and abuse of Lithuanian compatriots will be brought to account separately and punished accordingly. It is the duty of all good Lithuanians to take measures to arrest these Jews, and in grave cases, to mete out punishment..."

Thus the national rebellion of Lithuanian patriots very soon escalated into a wave of the anti-Semitic pogroms and distraction of the Jewish property, into unabated massacres, humiliations, tortures, and rapes.

Hundreds of Jews were killed on the streets and in their homes. Many were brought to the notorious seventh fort to face mass executions.

The pogroms started as early as June 25, first in the Kaunas neighborhood of Slobodka, in the towns of Plunge, Yurbarkas and Gardzai and then they spread to other places.

This first wave of violence had ended at the beginning of July. It was followed by a short period of calm during which all urban Jews were forced to move to the specially designated areas called ghettoes. However, starting from the middle of July, the violence re-emerged, this time in a more organized and planned fashion. Jewish residents of the villages and small towns in which the establishment of ghettoes tended to be impractical, were summarily executed by the so-called "police battalions" made up of local volunteers and supervised by the German SS officers.

Later, in October, Nazi administration, apart from the already existing small execution sites, established two major ones, the first one near the city of Kaunas — Ninth Fort, and another near Vilnius in Ponary forest.

Sites of mass executions in Lithuania:

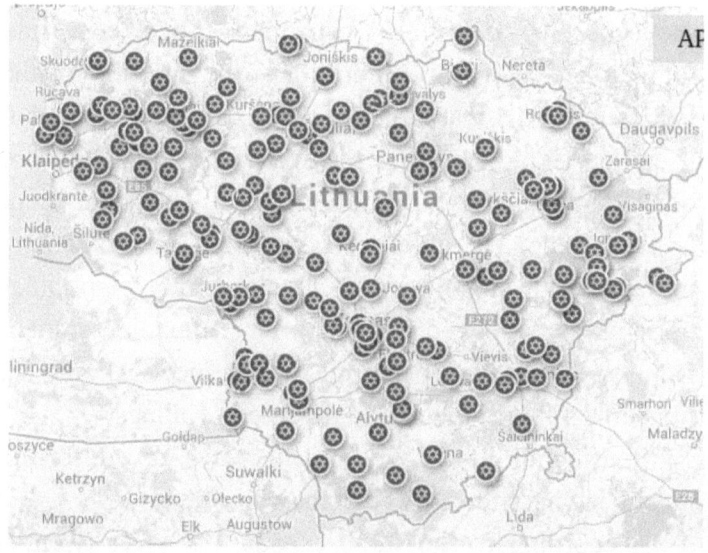

Overall, according to different estimates, between ninety and ninety five percent of Jews (the highest percentage in the whole of Europe) were killed in Lithuania during World War Two, for the most part by their former neighbors.

At the end of the war most of these killers escaped into the West where they found safe haven among the well-wishers, protected from the rightful punishment by the iron curtain of suspicion and ignorance.

Some of them (the smaller part) joined "forest brothers" — Lithuanian nationalist guerilla fighters who battled Soviet Union for the liberation of their homeland. Once again the Soviet secret police (this time the KGB) used tough and cruel measures to suppress the movement, once again trains with thousands of deportees began to move east into uninhabited parts of Siberia. By the middle of the Fifties the KGB was finally able to quell the rebels but it couldn't eradicate the free spirit and zealous desire of the Lithuanian population to live in an independent and free state. The quiet resistance continued for many more years, sometimes exploding into a popular uprising as happened in 1972 after Lithuanian student Romas Kalanta, protesting Soviet occupation, set himself on fire in the central square in Kaunas.

During all these developments Jews stayed, for the most part, neutral: it was not their business.

According to the 1970 census, just over twenty-three thousand Jews lived in the territory of Lithuania among two and half million Gentiles: close to eighteen thousand of them lived in the city of Vilnius, between four and five thousand in the city of Kaunas and the rest in the other places.

Two thirds were local Jews, called Litvaks: they were mainly Holocaust survivors and their children and represented the entire spectrum of the society — from doctors to butchers, from taxi drivers to artisans and craftsmen. At home they spoke Yiddish, celebrated Jewish holidays, kept up with the Jewish traditions and never felt ashamed of their Jewish identity. The sizable number of Litvaks was also involved in the illegal, according to the Soviet laws, business activities.

The other one third were Russian Jews, those who moved to Lithuania after World War Two. Contrary to the first group, they didn't know Yiddish, lost all links to Judaism and Jewish traditions and felt quite uncomfortable if someone reminded them of their ancestry. Their main connection to the "Yiddishkeit" was the fifth line in their internal passports (which stated a person's ethnicity) plus Jewish surnames and Semitic features of their faces which were difficult to hide. Many of them were coming from the mixed and intermarriage families while, at the same time, the majority represented the most educated part of the general population. Naturally, they nurtured the same mindset among their children, utterly convinced that only pre-eminence in some, certain field of activity, can guarantee a Jew the rightful place under the sun. On the other hand, due to their high position on the social ladder, they often behaved quite snobbishly and pretentiously. You could hear from them left and right: "my son just received his PhD in physics", or "my daughter has just been awarded the first prize in piano competition" and so on. It was inconceivable for these parents to have a child without a college degree.

I don't know the reason for such profound dissimilarity between these two groups. It could come from the fact that Russian Jews lived much longer under communist rule or because of the difference in the attitude among ethnic Russians and Lithuanians toward their Jewish compatriots.

Well, there was among us also, a third, very small, group of Jews, so called "hybrids", those, who had one parent coming from the Litvak side and another from "Russians". These Jews combined both traits: they valued good education as much as Russian Jews did and at the same time they kept Jewish traditions and customs as Litvaks.

Now, after the short introduction into the history of Lithuania let's return to my recollections of that wonderful autumn evening in the tiny courtyard of Kaunas synagogue.

The Yiddish amateur theatre

Finally, the earth has sunk into the moonlighted abyss and the first star, lonely and dazzling, abruptly emerged from the dark depths of the universe. We are now walking toward the building and the sound of the rustling leaves adds a distinct charm to this special occasion. The day of a judgment, the day of the divine intervention has begun.

We are taking the seats in the rear of the building, behind those pious congregants who, unlike us, know how to pray in Hebrew; the "frume idn" as Mikhail calls them. They know the procedure by heart. They learned it when they were still small kids, before World War Two. During that war the Nazis murdered all our rabbis and Soviet authorities closed all our yeshivas and those Jews who survived the slaughter but nevertheless remained faithful to the religion of their ancestors, must rely on memories from their childhood for there is nobody who could guide them through the complicated maze of prayers and rituals.

A short and lame man, by the name of Chaim Tsypkin, approaches the wooden cabinet mounted on the eastern wall of the synagogue. He slowly opens it revealing to the audience an old scroll of Torah, the other miracle survivor from the unprecedented calamity. All the congregants get up from their seats to show their respect to the old yellowish parchment.

"Three thousand years ago," Mikhail explains to us, "people didn't have books and didn't have paper and they had to write the words of the Torah on the parchment like this. But not everybody could afford to own it in his or her house. And the dwellers of some village (or maybe it was a town) came up with the great idea: they collected money from all the residents and bought one scroll for everybody. However, it was quite difficult for them to share it in privacy, and they decided to read it in public, aloud, so that everyone could hear the wise words of Torah simultaneously. But when could they do it? In those days people worked from morning till night and the only good time for reading was on the day of rest — either Saturday or holiday. They kept this scroll in the town's meeting house or "Beit Knesset" as it is called in Hebrew or a synagogue, as it was translated later to Greek. That is how the practice of reading the Torah in the house of prayers on Saturdays and holidays became a tradition."

I don't know if Mikhail has read this explanation somewhere or if he came to it by himself, but it sounds to me quite logical. Not everything he says is correct though, since he gained his knowledge from random books and centuries' old encyclopedias that he manages to find in the antique stores and in private collections. Then he fills in the missing parts with his own interpretations and guesses.

"Why do Jewish holidays always start in the evening?" inquires one of his disciples, a gloomy and unassuming guy by the name of Sergey, "and not the same for all normal people at midnight?"

Mikhail smiles condescendingly, showing us two rows of his rotten, crooked teeth. He knows all the answers to all the questions.

"I gave you the book of the Bible," he reminds Sergey. "Do you remember the beginning of it?"

And seeing expression of confusion in Sergey's eyes he recites the words he knows by heart:

"At the beginning God created the heavens and the earth. And the earth was empty and dark, and the Divine Presence hovered upon it. And God said: "let there be the light". And he saw that the light was good. And then he separated the light from the darkness and named it a day, while the cold darkness he named a night. And it was evening, and it was morning: the first day."

"What was first then?" enquires Mikhail in the same authoritative tone. "Night or day? It was evening… Right? That is why in our calendar each new day (not just a holiday) starts from the evening. Why 'normal people' start it at midnight puzzles me too."

I notice the expression of pride and veneration in Sergey's eyes. No wonder he is the best of Michael's students.

"How pathetic this whole thing is," remarks another member of our group, a tall and handsome guy in the black leather jacket, Todik Snyder, after he makes a fastidious observation of the synagogue's interior and the people inside it. "Once I visited Catholic church and everything there looked much more impressive and lavish."

I don't understand why Todik (behind his back we call him simply Pimple) joined our company. He does not seem to belong here: he is a pompous and flamboyant guy, arrogant and self-centered, constantly craving for everybody's attention and admiration. His main interests include body building, gambling card games and pretty girls and since he has a muscular body. He can play a little bit on guitar and knows a number of trivial jokes and he has a bountiful success among the representatives of the "weaker sex".

Although we are of the same age and lived our entire lives in the city of Kaunas, we hadn't met each other for a very long time. Our first encounter took place only last year during the rehearsal practice of the chorus, of which I was a member.

This chorus, by the way, represented a part of the, so-called, Yiddish amateur theatre — a unique and bizarre institution among all Soviet organizations. Well, there was also another similar theatre in the neighboring city of Vilnius, the capital of Lithuania, and we competed with each other —two black sheep in the sea of the otherwise homogeneous cultural establishment.

For the Lithuanian authorities it was the way to show Moscow comrades that they could act independently and not follow the directions of their mentors: see, you there, in Russia, are forbidding any development of the Jewish culture but we here, in Lithuania, are allowing it; we don't obey your orders. Similar rebellions came also from Latvian and Moldavian communists, but they were less lucky. Or maybe they just didn't have the same strength of will.

But going back to Todik. It was Nathan Frenkel, a younger brother of Mikhail's friend Abram Frenkel and theatre's long-time veteran, who brought him in.

"Would you like to join our dancing group? he once asked Todik during their usual beer party in the students' dormitory. "We desperately need male dancers."

"Of course not," answered a half-drunken Todik. "Who do you think I am — an idiot? I have other, much more important things to do."

"What are those important things?" wondered Nathan, "Have you seen our girls, dude? They all are incredibly sexy ballerinas. When you see their legs, my friend, you will forget all other things. I can guarantee you."

The last argument worked very well and the next day Todik came for the audition. The director of the dance troupe, Saevich-the-Elder, showed him a few simple movements and asked him to repeat them. And

Todik did. Then Saevich showed him a few more steps and Todik repeated them as well. Then Saevich said to him: "I am sure you will be a very good singer. Our chorus also needs talented people. I will recommend you to the chorus manager Isaac Abramovich Zingerman."

That is how Todik got in the theatre's chorus. The girls in the chorus were no match for the dancers and he was ready to leave it at once, but something held him back. That something was the music, the lovely Yiddish folk songs, these sad and jolly melodies that were born out of the anguish and faith of the suffering people.

Todik isn't a thin-skinned or sensitive person, particularly toward old and unfashionable rhythms. And therefore, his unexpected interest in our cultural enterprise came to all of us as a total surprise. But on the other hand, we didn't know then all the details and consequences of his life either.

Isaac Abramovich was playing on the piano when Todik walked into the room.

"Are you our new member?" he asked Todik without interrupting his play. "What is your first name, my friend?"

But Todik didn't answer. Perhaps for the first time in his life he was stunned by a harmony of sounds for he suddenly recognized this long-forgotten melody: it was the song his late mother sang to him many years ago when he was still a small child. And he suddenly remembered all those happy old days: his cozy crib, his mom's warm smile, and her low, pleasant voice...

The play abruptly stopped; Isaac Abramovich took his hands off the piano and looked directly at Todik's face. And we all, the members of the chorus, stared at him from the dark space behind our manager, all with a similar curiosity.

"What is the name of the song that you just played?" Todik asked Mr Zingerman regaining his consciousness.

"It was '*Rozinkes mit mandlen*', raisins with almonds, the old Jewish lullaby," answered Isaac Abramovich. "Have you heard this melody before? Now sing after me: "Unter yingele videle shteit a klor vaise tsigale..."

"A baritone," he concluded after hearing Todik's muffled mumblings, "Take a seat on the right-hand side but not at the very end."

Our chorus met twice a week, at evenings, after regular work hours. During the day, its participants had different types of activities. Isaac Abramovich Zingerman, for example, was a teacher of music in one of the city's middle schools, Todik studied civil engineering and Maya was still a high school student. We all were different people with different temperaments, different attitudes, talents and goals. Nevertheless, at nights, when we gathered in the small room of the trade union building, we were becoming just like one unified body mystically bonded by the magical power of music. These meetings created in us a sense of the community, a sense of common purpose and common destiny; a great feeling of being one big family.

The Yiddish theatre practiced in winter and performed during the summer months. Since the Soviet authorities didn't allow us to travel beyond Lithuanian borders, the theatre performed only in four places, one concert in each: in two cities — Kaunas and Vilnius and two resort towns — Palanga and Druskinikai.

The coastal town of Palanga located on the shore of the frigid and stormy Baltic Sea, was a real gem. It had wide sandy beaches, posh restaurants and many night clubs; it was elegant, stylish and noisy and very popular among those residents of Lithuania who could not afford the warmer and less rainy climate of the Crimean Peninsula in the south of Russia. Many vacationers there were either our friends, or our relatives, or our co-workers and therefore it wasn't a big surprise for us to see them during our concerts among the animated and supportive crowd.

Druskininkai, on the other hand, was a different kind of settlement. It was a small sleepy town, almost a village, situated in the middle of the pine tree forest and famous for its therapeutic mud and mineral water "Birute". The contingent of vacationers there was also different: most of them were convalescents and families with small kids and they were coming from the big cities outside Lithuania, such as Moscow,

Minsk and Leningrad to enjoy the fresh air, the magic power of the mineral water and the unfamiliar lifestyle. Druskininkai was offering them fewer red flags but more goodies in stores, neatly made spa facilities and polite service in public places and restaurants.

Well, the statement about the mineral water I may take back because this mysterious liquid had quite an unpleasant smell and even more unpleasant taste. And to add insult to injury it was warmed to the room temperature prior to consumption. Nevertheless, people with different types of stomach problems sipped it unwaveringly three times a day and all claimed miraculous cure. I bet they were misled by the oblivious notion that every product with an awful taste must be awfully healthy. Or otherwise — why would it exist in the first place?

The concert in Druskininkai fell on the last Sunday of July. It was the pinnacle of the vacation season, and the town was swarming with loitering and dawdling vacationers. But even under such circumstances we didn't expect to see such huge numbers of spectators packed into an unpretentious hall of the local trade union building. People stood by the doors and along the passages, at the stairs leading to the stage and even behind the windows — those unlucky ones who couldn't get even a standing ticket.

Poor Russian Jews — for many years they were deprived of their religion and customs. They were the outcasts, an anomaly, an odd group of people without their own place on earth, without history, language, and traditions, the "rootless cosmopolites" as they've been described by the official media and the "leeches on the healthy Slavic soul" — by the unofficial anti-Semites. The word "Jew" became a swear word: one of those words people used to curse each other. Even striving to be the first and the best didn't help them very much. But here, in Druskininkai, on the last Sunday of July Russian Jews discovered something else about themselves, something that deserved their admiration rather than shame; a pride rather than a pity, something they always had but were not aware of — they discovered their heritage.

After the concert, many enchanted spectators gathered outside the building to express to us their deep appreciation and gratitude. Several openly wept unable to hold their emotions. Others asked millions of questions about Jewish life in Lithuania, about Yiddish culture, political climate and the theatre itself: how it came into existence, when and what were the plans for the future and so on.

It was incredibly pleasant for us to realize that our hard work was not wasted, that it changed someone's life in a more meaningful and affirmative way. We felt a great satisfaction, quite similar to the one that a doctor might feel toward the recovery of a mortally ill patient.

One of the spectators, an old man, probably in his fifties or maybe even sixties, was especially thrilled.

Unlike others, he spoke to us in perfect Yiddish:

"I am a deputy chief editor of the central magazine *Ogonyok* in Moscow," he said. "My name is Cesar Solodar. I came here specifically to see your concert. For many years I hadn't heard Yiddish language or listened to Jewish songs. Someone in Moscow told me about your group but I didn't believe him. Now I can see that I was wrong. It was such a great pleasure to hear and to speak once again my mother tongue. Why don't you come to perform in our capital, in Moscow? You would have tremendous success there. I can guarantee you."

"As far as we are aware, the authorities in Moscow don't allow us to perform outside Lithuania," Isaac Abramovich answered for us all.

"This is nonsense," The strange man disagreed with him, "Our communist party has a principle of promoting diversity among all ethnic groups. We, communists, are internationalists. Nobody has the right to discriminate against anybody in our country. I will take care of this. It will be changed — trust me. Please give me your address. I will let you know of any progress."

Who was this awkward person, we wondered on our trip back to Kaunas. Was he a KGB provocateur or just a brainwashed lunatic who recently fell from the moon?"

But then the summer ended, and we began to prepare for the new theatrical season and forgot about the strange man and everything he had promised us that evening.

It was already the middle of December when Isaac Abramovich came at our usual practice time with a big smile on his face.

"I have terrific news," he announced. "Do you remember the man we met this summer after our concert in Druskeninkai — the one from the *Ogonyok* magazine? Well, yesterday I received a letter from him. Apparently, he kept his word. He indeed spoke about us to some high-ranking officials in Moscow. Well, they didn't agree yet to give us permission to perform in the other cities of the Soviet Union; they said such decisions should be coordinated with the local authorities. However, they came up with a better idea: they want to make a documentary movie about our theatre and the one in Vilnius and then show it on TV first central channel. Every person in the USSR will have a chance to see our performance, to hear lovely Yiddish songs and to watch our dances. Isn't this great?"

His words, however, were met with profound silence. Not everybody shared his excitement.

"It sounds quite fishy," replied someone from the back of the room, "Since when did the communist party become so much interested in promoting Jewish culture?"

"Maybe they finally woke up,," said Isaac Abramovich.

But we didn't let him finish the sentence. A commotion broke out after his first words and everyone began to shout and scream and not listen to each other. Among all of us only Todik seemed to be maintaining his composure, just occasionally throwing in his short caustic remarks.

"Listen, guys!" shouted, the usually unobtrusive and discreet Sergey. "They certainly will never show this movie on central TV. It will be shown only to western audiences, to demonstrate how wonderful Jewish life in USSR is and to convince naïve people in the west that there is no discrimination of Jews in the Soviet Union. Just look, we have unambiguous evidence of thriving Jewish culture in Kaunas…"

"Isn't it true?" interrupted Todik, "Don't we have a Jewish theatre in Kaunas?"

"Yes, but they don't allow us to sing Hebrew songs," said Maya joining the debate.

"It is because we are Yiddish theatre and not a Hebrew one," parried Todik.

"Guys, guys!" screamed Sergey. "You are crazy. This is not a time for silly jokes. Don't you understand that Soviet authorities want to use us as a tool for their disgusting propaganda tricks. They want to deceive people in the west and convince them that American Jews, who are fighting now for our right to emigrate, are simply liars and do not deserve to be trusted. No, no, we must refuse to participate in this propaganda show…"

"I'm afraid you can't," boomed Isaac Abramovich, once again taking the initiative. "The film crew has already left Moscow and it is on its way to Kaunas. It will be here either tomorrow or the day after t and they will start filming our reversals whether we want it or not."

As it happened just a few minutes earlier, his words were met with deaf silence but then as before, the intense stillness was replaced with the same vigorous uproar.

The general attitude was that in such a cas we should quit the theatre.

"No, you can't do it. You will all regret it," shouted a dismayed Isaac Abramovich. "We put so much effort in establishing this theatre. We did it against all odds and predictions and only because so many people made so many sacrifices. Don't destroy their dreams; don't destroy our theatre. Think about the consequences. You yourself enjoyed it. And do you remember how joyful were Russian Jews watching and listening to us in Druskininkai? I agree with you: not everything is okay in the Soviet Union; that is true. But our theatre is trying to make things better. We want Russian Jews to be proud of their traditions; we want them to know their own culture. You cannot be such callous people…"

He was a passionate fellow, this Isaac Abramovich, the director of our chorus, but he wasn't right. We did care about Jews from Moscow and

Leningrad and Minsk; we had to weigh all the options and make a choice and it wasn't on their side. Unfortunately for them. Well, on the other hand, we didn't know then that just several years later when thousands and thousands of Russian Jews would immigrate to Israel they would embrace not Yiddish language and culture but everything Russian. Russian language and Russian traditions embrace them as their own in a bizarre transformation from being Jews among Russians to becoming Russians among Jews.

As to the fate of the Yiddish Amateur Theatre — this event didn't mark its end either. The theatre ceased to exist but only temporarily. Later on it would be resurrected in Israel thanks to the efforts of many dedicated devotees such as Saevich-the-Elder, Isaac Abramovich and others and would be renamed "Anahnu Kan", which means "We Are Here." It will travel around the world to give performances in many places, in the cities of New York, Toronto, Berlin and Tel-Aviv, everywhere with consistent and immense success. However, you won't be able to see Russian Jews among the audience, nor anyone will be crying after the concerts as happened some time ago in the small Lithuanian town of Druskininkai.

"Not a big deal," Mikhail would say. "Both Yiddish and Russian are the languages of our galut, the languages of oppression and homelessness. Our children will soon forget them just as the children of the Egyptian slaves, our ancestors, forgot the language of the country of their birth once they settled in the Holy Land more than three thousand years ago.

The *Amateur Jewish Theatre (city of Kaunas)*

The claws of KGB

It is chilly and damp inside the synagogue as the congregation saves on the hefty heating bills. A stately cantor, wearing a worn-out "yarmulke" and tallit over his mink fur coat with the frayed sleeves, begins to chant the beautiful melody of Kol Nidre. But in the back, away from the pulpit, we can hardly hear his voice. The new arrivals, those who prefer to come under the cover of the night, the members of the communist party, directors of big corporations, agnostics and atheists make a lot of noise. They didn't have a chance to discuss the world news earlier, before the service started, and therefore ought to do it during the time of prayers. But why would they listen to the cantor anyway? They are certain that their presence in the synagogue on such a holy day is a mitzvah by itself. And a lot of a courage as well for there is no doubt that quite few of our co-congregants, who are now asking God to forgive them their sins and transgressions, will report tomorrow to Major Sidorchuk the names of the participants of tonight's service, trying not to miss anybody.

Yes, for sure there are KGB informers among the members of our congregation, and we are aware of them. We are looking for these snitches everywhere and all the time for we need to identify them well before they could become our friends, well before they can gain our trust and be promoted to our confidants because in the society, which is based on lies, eavesdropping gadgets and grotesque laws, friendship remains one of the very few traits that are still treasured and cherished as nothing else.

I am glancing around and here they are, our wise and knowledgeable "melamed" "reb" Mikhail, uncommunicative and somber Sergey, then Pimple, the Frenkel brothers... only Maya is missing — she is upstairs with the other women.

These are my acquaintances and friends, the dearest of my people, each one with his or her own mentality, disposition, attractive and annoying traits. We have been together for a long time. Together we shared a lot of anguish and a lot of joys, together lamented our losses and celebrated our accomplishments, cried and laughed and therefore it is so difficult for me to comprehend how one of them could be a traitor, a disgusting informer, a snitch, who wants to stab me at the back, to destroy my life and my future. And here comes the question — who could that loathsome person be? How can I find him and what should I do to prevent him from materializing his malevolent intentions?

These are very disturbing thoughts. Very, very disturbing. They never bothered me before not until recently. To be precise — not until last Tuesday when I was unexpectedly summoned to the local KGB office.

The day earlier, in the morning, a messenger knocked at the door to my apartment. He delivered me a writ.

"Tomorrow," he said, "precisely at nine o'clock, you must report to the guard at the entrance to the main KGB office. You are not allowed to have an excuse. You also are not allowed to disclose the nature of my visit to anybody, even to your parents. Sign here that you received the subpoena and understood my instructions. I cannot go back without your signature."

This sudden request and the way it had been delivered, swung my mood from the cheerful morning expectations to the state of intensive trepidation and anxiety. All day long I was trying to figure out what I did recently to raise the attention of that sinister organization. Is this an indication that Major Sidorchuk's silly threats are finally coming to fruition? Could it be my participation in Hebrew classes? If yes, then why so suddenly? I had been attending those classes now for more than a year. What else did I do lately?

And after giving some thoughts I concluded that it must be down to the letter which I signed several weeks ago.

This letter was an appeal of the Soviet Jews to the United Nations Human Rights Committee and to the

American Congress to help them to emigrate from the Soviet Union to Israel.

Mikhail brought it from Moscow in the middle of August and then, together with Sergey and Maya, he went through the apartments of the, known to us, local Jews soliciting them to sign the petition. He also asked me to help him, but I wisely refused, citing as the reason, my upcoming exams to the school of engineering. Now I could see how prudent and wise my decision was. Although signing the letter was still a risky act (there was a possibility that I might be expelled from the university for life and never become an engineer) it was much less dangerous than to urge others to sign it. Indeed, the authorities could define such activities as an anti-Soviet agitation and propaganda and sentence the perpetrator to a lengthy term in prison.

This letter was not unique though. In those days, a number of similar letters circulated occasionally among Jews of the Soviet Union. In these letters anonymous authors expressed their deep attachment to the land of Israel, stating their desire to move to the birthplace of their ancestors and appealing to the international community and different human rights organizations for help.

Here is an example of one such letter:.

"If I will forget you, oh Jerusalem," it passionately proclaimed, "let my right hand forget its skill, let my tongue stick to the roof of my mouth, if I do

not remember you, if I do not set you above my highest joy!

For two thousand years our ancestors lived in exile. Homeless, deprived from the basic human rights, mistreated, and despised by their hosts, they moved from one place to another in a search for safety and fair treatment. At certain moments of time one or another compassionate nation was offering them a temporary refuge. But such lulls never lasted for too long. Envy, ignorance, intolerance to anything different and other human deficiencies always found the way to end this relative tranquillity. And Jews once again were accused of causing natural disasters and spreading infectious diseases; of committing ritual murders and practicing cruel usury. And then one expulsion was followed by another; one massacre was followed by several more. Calamities and sufferings pursued our forefathers on their journey through the places and times. But every year, during the annual Passover Seder, they were turning into the direction of their ancient homeland, repeating these words again and again:

"The next year we will be in Jerusalem."

The miracle had happened: like a phoenix the nation was reborn from the ashes. We didn't forget Jerusalem and she needs our hands. Once again, like two thousand years ago, we ourselves can preside over our destiny and don't depend on someone's good will.

It is the right of every human to choose for himself

the place where he wants to live. Please, help us to convince Soviet authorities to respect our rights."

That is how most of those letters sounded.

This is the example of the signatures under the letter addressed to the UN. People had to give their full names and addresses, so there wouldn't be any questions regarding authenticity of the petition.

We didn't know who wrote them. We knew some people who distributed them, we knew those who passed them around and those, who decided to sign under such petition, clearly indicating his or her full name and address to eliminate any doubt in the authenticity of the signatures, but at the same time, inadvertently, helping KGB officials to uncover the identities of the signatories.

Soviet bureaucrats saw these petitions and letters as a threat to their authority, as a slander on the "socialist way of living" and as a critique of their authoritarian rule. It was inconceivable for them why someone, in his clear mind, could prefer a "rotten capitalist society" over the one ruled by the communist party, "workers' paradise"? They saw such petitions as an ultimate betrayal of their ideals.

During its covert journey each of these letters could be seized by the various KGB agents at any time and in any place and then everyone involved in this venture could face quite unpleasant consequences: from the expulsion from his or her workplace to losing his or her life. The most dangerous part in this clandestine operation fell on the shoulders of several dedicated Zionists from Moscow, on people like Vladimir Slepak and his wife Maria, on Yosef Begun, Ida Nudel, Nathan Sharansky and several others. These brave men and women took the task and responsibility of delivering the petitions to the foreign tourists, mostly American or British Jews, and sometimes, to the diplomats from the Dutch Embassy, which represented at that time Israeli interests in the USSR. Such activities in the Soviet Union were classified as acts of high treason and typically led to extremely severe punishments. And indeed, many of those, mentioned above, Zionists spent countless years in putrid cells of Moscow prisons and in Siberian labor camps, and one of them, Nathan Sharansky, even received a death penalty.

As for American and British tourists — they also faced significant danger for they had to smuggle these letters out of the Soviet Union into the West.

No doubt that some curiously minded individual may rightfully ask: what was the purpose of their efforts? Why were there people in Russia, USA, Canada and Great Britain who choose to risk their lives, careers and future for the simple piece of paper? Was it, really, worth it?

Mikhail explained to us that the intention was to inform the world outside USSR, to tell it, that not only a few disgusting renegades, as Moscow officials relentlessly claimed, but the entire Jewish community of Russia was eager to leave the "people's paradise" and exchange it for some other place on earth.

"We don't have the power to fight this evil empire directly: it has secret police, an enormous army and a lot of prison wards," he said, "Besides, we are just a small minority among the Soviet population and therefore the only weapon we have is to tell people the truth. With the help of American Jews, we may break that nasty iron wall, which surrounds us and settles on the land of our ancestors, in Israel."

Israel in those days was not just a point of destination. Like a beacon, like a lighthouse which, during the darkness of the night, directs desperate sailors to a safe harbor, it was guiding Russian Jews from the misery of their oppressive reality toward beautiful life without tyranny and discrimination.

Eventually the emotional appeal of the Soviet Jews triggered mass movements in the USA and in other countries in support of their plight and helped them to break the wall Mikhail so passionately was talking about.

These events, however, occurred much later, several years after I received, as mentioned above, a subpoena to come to the city's main KGB office. I had no clue then, no hint what to expect from this meeting or how my future might depend on it, and I was extremely anxious.

I remember the day of my visit to the KGB office very well, as if it happened just yesterday. It began in a bright sunny morning, cheerful and refreshing, the last spell of the departing summer. Although the smell of the approaching fall could already be felt in the air it was still quite vague and fragile. I was walking along the city's main thoroughfare with the ironic name "Alley of Liberty" toward the gray ugly building at the end of it and contemplating how I was going to act during the upcoming interrogation.

My previous experience in dealing with this infamous organization was limited to the infrequent encounters with Major Sidorchuk on the walkway between our houses. The present situation, however, was obviously different, more challenging and I had to consider various scenarios and to prepare myself for any surprising development. What questions they might ask me? Let's say, they will ask me how my signature appeared on the letter? How? What should I answer? Well, I can tell them that I found the letter accidentally on the table in the "Office for Visas and Emigration" on the day I came to apply for permission to emigrate to Israel, and I don't know who left it there and how it got there. I just signed it.

What else might they ask? Well, the number of possibilities was just enormous, and their likelihood drove me crazy. What should I do? How should I deal with it?

If Mikhail would be around, I would defy the promise I made to the KGB messenger and consult him on the strategy and guidance and possible consequences of the chosen path: Mikhail was an expert on such matters. Alas, he left the city a couple of days ago and didn't tell us when he is planning to come back.

Therefore, I had no other choice but to recall everything I read in articles and books about interrogations of the famous Russian revolutionaries and Soviet patriots during civil war and World War Two and rely on the authors' truthfulness in revealing their stories. And the best strategy I could derive from their narratives was to keep my mouth shut, and no matter what, but don't reveal anything that might cause trouble to my friends. Just pretend to be dumb and you cannot divulge any secret. The problem here was that in such cases the KGB could resort to more radical methods of interrogation, like torture, which made me feel sick to my stomach.

I would be even more frightened if I would know in advance that our meeting was instigated not by my old neighbor, Major Sidorchuk, but by the special KGB envoy from Moscow, who came here specifically to interrogate me. At least that was the tale Lieutenant Belousov told me when he introduced himself at the checkpoint to the entrance of that cursed edifice.

After several formalities, like verifying my identity, he led me upstairs, to the fourth floor. I had never been in this place before; I'd only heard rumors and scary stories and therefore the novelty and curiosity had pushed away my earlier fear. I was looking around myself trying to compare the picture I saw in front of me to the images I created in my imagination and quite soon I came to the conclusion that they didn't seem to differ too much.

We climbed up by the spiral marble stairway and at every landing I noticed a metal mesh stretched between the links, blocking the gap in the middle. It looked as if someone put it on purpose to prevent people from committing suicide in case someone decided to jump down between the links.

"The KGB doesn't do such things without the reason," I was telling myself. "There were probably instances when the prisoners preferred to jump down to their imminent deaths rather than face the upcoming torture. It meant they had been tortured here pretty badly."

The old anxiety came back. I caught myself thinking that I had no idea what might happen to me later today: would I be eventually released and go home to see my parents, or would I be sent directly to a prison without saying even one word to them? How does the KGB deal with such stuff? Are they going to torture me? And if "yes" then how badly? I was imagining an excruciating pain, needles under my fingernails, slowly broken bones, electrical shocks…. Would I be able to withstand all this abuse and remain mute? Would I have enough courage to keep my mouth shut and not reveal my friends? To my great embarrassment I had to admit to myself that I wasn't sure. I wasn't sure if I could be strong enough to endure all this pain. And on the way up I was repeating to myself again and again: "You must be stubborn; you must be strong."

"We don't torture people here," explained Lieutenant Belousov as soon as we took our seats across the dark brown table in the equally murky room.

Behind the lieutenant's back was a small, grated window and in it I saw the well of the building's courtyard, also dark and depressing just like the room we were sitting in.

"These are just the myths perpetrated by the dishonest capitalist propaganda," he assured me authoritatively, noticing the expression on my face, "Such excessive methods were used a long time ago, during Stalin's times. It is not the case any more. Do not listen to the lies of the "Voice of America"."

Then he began to ask me some questions, very trivial ones, like the date of my birthday or the names of my classmates from the fifth grade. Not to answer would be quite silly. He wrote all my responses on the sheets of paper and I had to sign on the bottom of each one to assure that what he wrote was indeed the truth. It took him more than an hour to get to the point.

"Two weeks ago, on September the third," he said slightly raising his voice, "you had in your possession a Xerox copy of the illegal Zionist literature, a book called *Exodus*. Who gave it to you?"

His question caught me by surprise, I didn't expect to hear it and looked at him in amusement.

"Well, I can see by the expression on your face that you know what I am talking about," said my interrogator and smiled," so, who gave it to you?"

Who gave it to me? Pimple did. He gave it to me. I remembered the whole sequence of the events quite well.

It was the late evening, around nine o'clock or maybe even later. We — me, Sergey and Maya, were in the restaurant having coffee and ice cream during a heated debate with one of my classmates, Rimas (Rimantas). Rimas for some reason liked our company and often joined it to express his unconventional views which, in many cases, were diametrically opposite to ours. He was an ardent Lithuanian nationalist and fiercely defended the actions of his countrymen against all kinds of accusations, either they were right or wrong. Later, in the eighties, he became one of the founding members of the Lithuanian nationalist organization "Sajudis" which, against all odds, was able to drive the Soviet Union out of their country and bring, once again, independence and freedom to his beloved homeland.

The subject of our debate this time was the role of Lithuania in World War Two. We were trying to convince Rimas in Mikhail's theory that the Holocaust had started not in Germany, not somewhere else but right here, in Lithuania, due to the active participation of the local population in extermination of their Jewish neighbors. We choose Sergey to be our "spokesman."

"Look," he was saying to Rimas, "at the beginning, when the Nazis came to power, their attitude toward Jews was not extremely ferocious: boycotts of Jewish goods and financial institutions, dismissal of educators, intimidation, harassment… Their goal was to persuade Jews to leave the country and allow Germans to become a "pure Aryan nation". However, Nazi efforts were only marginally successful: Jews didn't leave Germany at the rate Nazis hoped they would. There were several reasons for this. First of all, the other countries, hurt by their own economic problems, didn't show any desire to accept the refugees who would become competitors in their already crowded job markets, and second, many German Jews remained loyal to their country despite their mistreatment."

"Typical Jewish attitude," remarked Rimas.

But Sergey, pretending he didn't hear the caustic remark, continued: "When the Nazis saw such dismal results of their efforts, they intensified their efforts and introduced in 1936 so called "Nuremberg laws", which stripped German Jews of their citizenship and imposed many other discriminating rules. These new measures were supposed to encourage Jews to leave Germany. By the spring of 1939 the Nazis almost achieved their goal and very few "untermensch" remained in their country. But then it was "Anschluss", a unification of Germany and Austria, and more than two hundred thousand Austrian Jews instantly became the new tenants of the "Third Reich". Such a turn of events forced the Nazis to change their means of persuasion..."

They ordered the wealthy Vienna Jews to clean the streets of the city.

"Hold it!" Rimas interrupted." You are wrong. Anschluss had happened in 1938, not in 1939."

"Oh, yes, you're probably right," Sergey corrected himself after a few seconds of mental deliberation, "Yes, I guess it indeed happen in 1938. But the actual date doesn't change much. The point is that from that time on the Nazis started to use force to achieve their goal. First, they forcibly deported seventeen thousand Jews with Polish passports to Poland. Poland refused to accept these poor deportees and they got stacked between two countries for months. And then came "Kristallnacht" and …"

"It meant that the Nazis had already begun to kill Jews at that time," interrupted Rimas.

"It was only a spontaneous killing," countered Sergey. "Not planned, not yet the Holocaust. Even when the Germans occupied Poland in 1939, they didn't start to kill Jews immediately. Surely, they were shocked by the new reality: despite all their efforts for almost seven years, the number of Jews in the Third Reich didn't decline but quite the opposite — it increased and increased dramatically: they got another three million Jews. At this point the Nazis realized they must do something dramatically different from what they had in the past if they indeed had any chance of achieving their goal. But what? First, they came up with the idea of transferring Jews to the island of Madagascar in the Indian Ocean. Correct? You know this, don't you? And you know that such a suggestion was quickly rejected on the grounds of its total impracticality. Other similar ideas popped up, all of them from the same realm of fantasy."

"Didn't they start to build Jewish ghettoes at that time already?" asked Rimas sarcastically.

"Sure they did. And not just for the purpose of segregation. They did it to be prepared for any potential development, (still unsure what it might be). The Nazis wanted to separate the Jews from the rest of the population because this would make them easier to deal with Jews later. In any case they were still far away from committing mass murders."

"I agree with you," said Rimas, "The Nazis at the beginning didn't plan to kill Jews. They were not those irrational Jew-killers, as some pseudo-historians try to portray them. They wanted to remove Jews only from the area they envisaged as an "Aryan living space" and had no intention of eliminating them from the face of the Earth in general. Of course, they could "understand" other anti-Semites, like Palestinian leader Al-Husayni, but his goal and goals of other lunatics never became their priority. Basically, the Nazis started to kill Jews only out of necessity, out of their inability to get rid of them in any other way. I agree with you. But what had Lithuanians got to do with it?"

"What? The massacres first started in the Baltic states and in western Ukraine in June of 1941, after the German invasion of the Soviet Union. And the perpetrators at the beginning were not the infamous Einsatzgruppen "death squads", as many historians mistakenly claim, but the local militia."

"Jews began to persecute Lithuanians first," snapped Rimas, "Before the war, the Soviet secret police, the NKVD, was full of Jews. They deported thousands of local Lithuanians to Siberia. The actions of the people's militia were in response to the actions of the NKVD and not necessarily directed against Jews."

"You could be right. The first executions which began in the last days of June were indeed directed mainly against communists and consequently at the Jewish members of the communist party. However these actions soon spread to the Jewish population in general and took a form of pogroms while the perpetrators were still local militiamen. Einsatzgruppen started to participate in mass executions only by the middle of July, if not later. Even more, at the beginning of July, the Nazi administration actually issued an order which, under the penalty of death, prohibited militiamen to kill Jews. In Lithuania, just like it happened previously in Poland, Jews were ordered to move to ghettoes. And that directive was indeed implemented in the big cities which had a significant Jewish population and the pogroms there had stopped. But there were also many small towns with only a handful of Jewish residents. It looked impractical to create a ghetto for just a couple of dozens of people. Transporting them to the larger cities hundred kilometers away when the German military desperately needed all means of transportation also didn't look like a good option. And then someone suggested (I don't know who): why not just to kill them? The local population was quite enthusiastic and sympathetic to the violence of mobs during earlier pogroms. Why would it object to the killings now? Thus the first mass murders started in the small towns and villages across Lithuania. Only at that point the Nazis realized: here it is — the long-sought solution to the "Jewish problem". And only then did the Einsatzgruppen come into action and extend the experience of the small towns to the entire territory."

"Don't tell me that Lithuanians are the biggest

anti-Semites in the world," started Rimas with the same degree of sarcasm but Maya interrupted him.

"Guys, look!" she shouted, "Pimple is here! He wants to tell us something!"

In the faraway corner of the restaurant Todik Sneider was frantically waving his hands, showing us all kinds of gestures, which supposedly meant: "Hey, guys, cut off your conversation and come to me".

Prior to this moment I had no idea that he was even present in the restaurant. Usually he was entering the premises strutting like a peacock, telling everyone left and right funny jokes, patting everyone's shoulders, laughing, and trying immediately to become the center of the common attention and enjoyment. But tonight, for whatever reason, he sneaked in like a frightened mouse and quietly took his place in the faraway corner, near the kitchen. He sat there, probably, for a quite a while (I don't know for how long) but after noticing the absence of the attention to his persona, he decided to reveal his presence in some other, more active way.

"What happened to him?" I asked Sergey and Maya, puzzled by the unusual behavior of our friend, "he acts very strangely today."

Sergey just shrugged; he also never saw Todik acting in this way.

"Something serious probably," suggested Maya who was always concerned about everything and everybody.

"Look," I said to our Lithuanian opponent Rimas, "we are sorry, but we need to quit our discussion now. Let's finish it some other time. Our friend is waiting for us".

Pimple indeed was waiting for us and waiting quite impatiently: he was in an unusual, agitated mood. We noticed how extremely anxious he was as soon as we approached his table. He nervously glanced at both sides, to assure himself that nobody was spying on him, made a conspiratorial expression on his face and loudly whispered: "Listen, guys. Say not one word, just follow me and I will show you something very-very interesting."

He led us to the furthest corner of the adjoining restaurant park and there, under the blurry light of the street lantern, he showed us a thick collection of the loose papers with the Xerox-copied text: the pages looked awful — most of the letters were faded and pale, smudged with the ugly blots of black ink.

"What is this?' I asked Todik, puzzled by the secrecy in which he showed us this stuff.

"It is a book," he answered proudly.

"What kind of a book? Where did you get it?'

"It is a novel," he said, "A fiction. It is called *Exodus*."

"Fiction? What fiction? What are you talking about? Who is the author?"

"I don't know who he is. Someone American. I think his name is Leon Uris. This is his Russian translation. Not English."

"But what is this book about?" asked Maya.

"It is about Jews, Zionists, you will like it. I got it for one day only. Tomorrow at eight in the morning I must return. So, you can have this book for almost ten hours. Don't waste your time."

And we didn't. The next nine and half hours we, me, Sergey and Maya, spent devouring the incredible story on the park's exfoliated and dilapidating bench, It was about a different kind of Jews, not those who cleaned on their knees the streets of the Austrian capital and not those who lived among us who got used to being routinely spat in their faces trying by all possible means to hide their Jewish identity. No, the Jews in the book were vastly different — they were proud of their Jewishness and eager to fight for their dignity and freedom.

We didn't care about inadequate lighting, cold weather and a brisk northerly wind nor were we worried about loitering hoodlums and drunkards. Neither the blurry script nor the tons of mistakes of the badly copied text bothered us either: the time passed like one single minute...

"So, who gave you the book?" repeated an impatient Lieutenant Belousov, now without even a hint of a smile.

"It would be quite unwise for you not to answer my question," he continued in a stern tone, "since you have already revealed to us a lot of information. And you cannot claim you don't remember what happened to you just two weeks ago if you remember the names of your classmates from the fifth grade."

He paused.

"Who betrayed me?" I thought frantically, "Who could commit such a despicable and treacherous act?"

"I noticed that you have been thinking," calmly continued Lieutenant Belousov, "you are an intelligent man; I can see that. We speak differently to the intelligent people than we do to the uneducated ones. To the intelligent person we speak frankly and straight. So, let me tell you frankly and straight that we don't care about you personally unless you try to hinder our efforts. It is not about you and even about the person who gave you that disgusting pamphlet. But the chain will eventually bring us to the original perpetrator. Why is this so important to us? Well, there are only a handful of Xerox copy machines in the Soviet Union and all of them are in the government offices. Not just in regular offices but in the special ones, very high up offices. Offices that contain government secrets. Do you understand this? Someone who works in one of those offices and has access to the Xerox machine used his or her position in the workplace to proliferate this anti-Soviet material. Then there was also someone who translated this ugly pamphlet into Russian. These are the people we are looking for. Do you understand? The crime of reading this illegal book by itself is not a big one. However, the crime of protecting those who disseminate such prohibited literature is huge. We are making, how to say it, a list of the individuals who are resisting to co-operate with us (for your information, there are only very few of such individuals). And once in a while we draw from that list several names and put those people on trial in order to stop others from similar anti-Soviet activities. To teach them, to give them a good lesson, so to speak. We have damaging files on everybody, including you. In the last several years you committed a number of serious offences and misdemeanors punishable by long prison terms and by hard labor at uranium mines. Your participation in spreading these illegal Zionist propaganda books is just one of them. On the other hand, we have a different list of people — a list of those who are helping us. Some of them, like you, want to leave our country. We say to them: good riddance. We have no objection. And since they are helping us, we may help them too. It is all mutual. Do you understand? Mutual. So, you, as an intelligent person, (if you are indeed an intelligent person) should carefully weigh all your options here: It is to have a loving family, big house in Manhattan or Chicago, own your own company in the Silicon Valley and have a lot of money while another option is many years of hard manual labor, humiliation, abuse and the high probability of being raped by the fellow inmates in a dirty camp somewhere in Siberia. Make a choice. It is all yours. Who, do you think, will appreciate your stubborn silence here? Ah? Who will even find out about it? Did such thoughts ever cross your mind? And who is the person you are trying to protect? Does he or she really deserve it? Ah? Do you really want to sacrifice your life and your future for his or her sake? Think about it; think very hard."

And I was thinking; I was thinking very hard, I was weighing all my options. On the one hand it was quite easy to say just one word. Just one word, just one name and everything would be over: no risk of going to prison but a high probability of getting out of the country. They will help, he promised. And nobody will ever find out. On the other hand... I will become a person I was disgusted with just a few minutes ago: a traitor, a snitch, a snake. A friend? How will I live the rest of my life with such sin on my shoulders? But then, is Todik indeed a man for whom I would want to sacrifice everything that I have? Is he indeed? Would he sacrifice his life for me, for example? Or, in fact, would anyone of my friends do it? How would they act in my place? Let's say, the same Pimple, Mikhail or even Maya? Maya? Well, Maya was a special case.

Maya Katz

Since her early childhood Maya Katz dreamed of becoming an artist: she drew pictures of pastures and trees, tempestuous waters and immaculate houses, animals and human beings. She drew them in color and in black and white, with oil and with charcoal, on canvases and on a simple drawing paper. She was ready to make a portrait of anyone willing to sit motionlessly for an hour or two. Once she drew my portrait as well and I still keep it among my most precious things, first — because I like my image, and secondly — because it, for good or for bad, is still the memory and thirdly — well, who knows, maybe one day she indeed will become a world celebrity.

After finishing high school, she applied for the College of Fine Arts in the hometown of the famous painter Marc Chagall, in the city of Vitebsk.

"Are you out of your mind?" asked Maya's father upon learning the news. "This is not an occupation for a woman. Not at all. You are going to be a medical nurse."

His older brother, the one who lives in Israel, had explained to him in a number of letters that a medical nurse was the most sought-after specialty among

Israeli women and since in the Soviet Union it required only two years of study and didn't cost any money it would be utterly stupid not to exploit such opportunity.

Maya's father respected his brother's opinion. He respected it for a very simple reason: because his brother was a smart man who had left Lithuania prior to Second World War.

"You should all come with me," he said then to the members of his family. "We will build in Palestine our own Jewish country where we'll be able to defend ourselves with the weapons against all our enemies."

His words, however, fell on deaf ears.

"We are not idiots," the members of his family answered him. "Why should we exchange the great climate and our comfortable lives here, in Lithuania, for the heat and dust and all kinds of perils in the strange land? We live in the middle of the twentieth century in the center of civilized Europe. Nothing bad will happen to us here."

None of those people are now alive except Maya's father but even he survived the slaughter because of an accident.

In the fall of 1943, he was transferred from Kaunas ghetto to a creepy military structure on the outskirts of the city called the Ninth Fort. During the time of Lithuanian independence, it served as a penitentiary for political prisoners. The Nazis transformed it to a death camp and for more than a year they were bringing Jews: first from Western

Europe, from Austria, Germany and Czechoslovakia and then the locals and murdering them in giant pits outside the building. But in 1943 the situation changed. The Red Army defeated the Wehrmacht in the battle of Stalingrad and was advancing toward Lithuania uncovering on its way the evidence of the unimaginable crimes. The time came to hide these crimes more thoroughly.

Maya's father shared his cell with another sixty-seven men and four women. The prisoners' task was to dig out earlier buried corpses, pile them up into gigantic pyramids, spray with the gasoline and burn. Unfortunately, not all parts of the human body could be destroyed in this way as the bones and skulls resisted the fire. Maya's father's job was to remove unburned parts from the ashes and crush them with the hummer into dust. And then he had to spread the dust over the field. It was a hard job and required a lot of stamina. However, the most disturbing part was not the physical exhaustion but the thought that one day he might come across the bones of his own parents or siblings. This thought drove him crazy.

As well, he and all other prisoners were certain that after finishing their job they all would share the fate of their predecessors: The Nazis had no plans to leave witnesses behind. It was just a matter of time before the prisoners themselves would become crushed bones and cold ashes — their tormentors had already decided their future. But nothing is certain in this world and to the Nazis' surprise, those condemned to death cheated their destiny and on the night of Christmas of 1943 made a daring escape.

After the war, in the late forties, Maya's father volunteered for a special NKVD unit called "the battalion of exterminators". It had the task of chasing in the woods, so called, "forest brothers" — the guerilla fighters who were fighting for the national independence of Lithuania. During the German occupation many of them joined Nazi death squads and actively participated in the slaughter of their Jewish neighbors. Maya's father felt he owed them the similar favor.

Most likely due to his service in this defunct KGB unit Soviet authorities now for many years had refused to grant his family an exit visa citing as the reason for the denial some unspecified security concerns.

"I don't know any secrets," he was telling Major Sidorchuk during their frequent encounters at the city's communist party meetings, "I don't understand what the problem is. I love my mother Russia and have no intention of hurting her. I just want to live together with my brother in Tel Aviv. That is all."

"In that case why don't you ask your brother to come here?" said a puzzled Major Sidorchuk, "Why can't both of you live in our country, in the beacon of freedom and equality among all nations of the world?"

By that time Maya's father also became a smart man, just like his older brother, and therefore he decided not to answer the question.

It is very possible that his past hardships and sufferings had made him a tough and uncompromising person, a tyrant to the members of his family. Or maybe he was born with such character. No one really knows but one way or another Maya has suffered a lot from his mistreatment.

Once, when she was still a freshman in college, a big event had happened in the Soviet Union: the famous painting of Leonardo Da Vinci *Mona Lisa* had arrived in Moscow to go on display in the Pushkin Museum of Fine Art. That was the time of the warming relations between USSR and France, and it was a French 'good will' gesture with the intention to promote just recently started detente. Since an "average" Soviet citizen had a zero chance to see this painting in Louvre, the queue to the exhibition by far exceeded the queue to the nearby Lenin Tomb. Even old revolutionaries and exemplary communists, mobilized for such an occasion by the government, gave their preference to the portrait of the young lady over the dead body of their deceased leader.

"Could I go to Moscow to see the exhibition?" Maya asked her father one evening, "It is once in a lifetime opportunity."

"Of course not," he said sternly, "First of all we don't have the money for such silly whims. And secondly, you don't need to go to Moscow to see it: just buy an illustrated book in our local bookstore."

"But this is not the same," Maya protested. "How could you compare the original painting to a poster?"

"Don't give me a hard time," he said visibly annoyed by her insistence, "When we are living in Israel and you are making a lot of money working as a nurse, then you could go anywhere you want, including Paris, and stare at your original as much as you wish."

"What if we will never live in Israel with the luck that we've had so far? For more than ten years we have been waiting to get the exit visa without any progress. How much longer can we wait for it? Is it possible for us to start living now and not postpone everything to the uncertain future? We won't be able to return the years we have been wasting for so long."

But her father didn't see the reason to continue the discussion. The "Voice of America" just started to broadcast on the radio the latest world news and his main priority became deciphering human speech from the irritating noise produced by the jamming stations.

Maya was in tears when I met her the next day.

"My father is a bastard," she said to me, "but I don't need him or his stupid money. I will earn myself and will travel to Moscow on my own will."

"How do you intend to accomplish that?" I asked her, "You will need a lot of money."

"Don't worry, I have a plan. First of all, I will skip my lunches in school. And then I will find a job. Our local bakery, for example, is looking for workers for the night shift. I'll do any job, manual, hard, whatever, but you will see. I will go to Moscow if not for anything else then just to show my dictatorial father that he cannot control me any more."

A couple of months later I bumped into her on Lenin Street near the movie theatre Planeta. She was heading toward the railroad station. Although it was already almost the end of June, it was still cold and gloomy, as if Mother Nature had mixed up the year's seasons, and the brisk northerly wind mercilessly nipped our ears. Nevertheless, Maya's face was beaming with such happiness that I'd never seen before.

"How are you doing?" I asked her, "I haven't seen you for a long time."

"I am leaving for Moscow," she said ignoring my question, "Remember what I told you some time ago, I was able to live to my promise. I have collected fifty-eight rubles to pay for the round-trip ticket and for the art exhibition. "

"Wow! You are kidding!" I was deeply surprised by the fact that such a nondescript and ordinary girl like Maya could be so strong and persistent. But then, having a second thought, I asked her cautiously, "Are you sure that fifty-eight rubles will be enough for you to cover all your expenses?'

"I am sure it will be enough," she said, "I think I will have enough money even to pay for the famous Tretyakov gallery. Since my childhood I dreamt of visiting it and see the original works of the great Russian artists: Repin, Kuindzhi, Levitan. Now I finally have the opportunity to realize that dream and I am very, very happy. Of course, I could try to collect more money to be on the safe side, but I don't have much time: the exhibition will be closing next Monday. This is my last chance to see it."

"Then, what about food? Will you have enough money to pay for the food?"

"Oh, food is not a problem." Maya was smiling once again; "I got used to skipping my lunches. Now I am going to skip my dinners as well. This is not a big deal. It will be good for my body. And after all, it is just for one week only — I will survive."

"And what about your lodgings then?" I continued my interrogation.

"What about it?"

"How are you going to pay for the place you plan to stay?"

"Oh, that! It won't be necessary. This is, actually, the best part of my trip," she crowed. "Mikhail had arranged for me to stay at the Slepaks' apartment. Have you heard about them? Of course, you did. They are the legends, the prisoners of Zion. And they strongly insisted, when I called them, that I shouldn't pay anything for staying in their place. They said it is their obligation to help other Jews. I am just bringing them a book as appreciation for their hospitality."

She showed me the book: *The history of the Jews*

in Russia and Poland by Simon Dubnov, published in Riga in 1932.

"I bought it in our local bookstore which sells used books," she boasted, "People in the store have no idea how much it might cost: I paid just one ruble. Could you imagine? I hope the Slepaks will like it. What do you think?"

"I am sure they will. It is indeed a rare book, collectible."

"That is what I thought, but there is something else, something you would not even guess. In a couple of days Slepaks will hold a seminar in their apartment. It will be dedicated to the presentation of Jews in the Soviet and Russian literature and many famous writers and dissidents are supposed to attend it. Take your breath: Okudzava, Voinovich, maybe even Solzhenitsyn... I never even dreamt I would be present at such an event and I am really looking forward to it."

In the old days we didn't have cell phones, but we still needed to be "connected". For this purpose we employed the hall of the unpretentious restaurant with the voguish name "Coffee and Ice-cream". For a fraction of a ruble you could spend hours sipping a bitter over-burnt coffee and participating in the endless discussions with the other college students about all aspects of human life: from politics, to movies, to literature. This place had an even wider purpose: it functioned as an information booth for if you were looking for somebody but couldn't find him or her, you would come there and make an inquiry and it was guaranteed someone would know the whereabouts of the missing person

So, the next morning Todik Snyder found me in the restaurant at my usual place near the window.

"Wow, how lucky I am," he yelled from another side of the hall while still strolling toward me "that I found you here."

"I am glad to hear that," I responded.

"Well, to tell you the truth, I wasn't looking for you," he corrected himself. "I was looking for Maya. I called her at home, but no one answered."

"She is in Moscow."

"Ah, that is why… look, could you do me a favor? I am leaving tomorrow "for potatoes". You know, the usual shit. Every year the same one: our college administration sends us to the farms to help kolkhozniks to plant and collect vegetables. Now we are going to a collective farm near Aregala and I won't be back for three weeks or maybe even longer. But I owe Maya money and I want to return it as soon as possible. Could you give it to her when she's back from Moscow?"

"Of course. Not a problem."

He handed me a bundle of soiled bills.

"Here," he said, "Fifty-eight rubles. You don't need to count them."

"Fifty-eight? So many? When did you get them?"

"Yesterday," he said and chuckled. "Oh, it was

quite a story! Listen. Last night me and my girlfriend, Grazina, (you know her) were at the railroad station: she was going back to her village. Her dad recently broke a leg and is staying at home. He asked her to pick up from his employer his last two weeks' salary: seventy rubles, overall. And that's what she did. But later, at the railroad station, when she looked in her purse, she couldn't find the money. We couldn't find it anywhere. Grazina panicked. She said her father was going to kill her for it was almost a half of their monthly family budget. How are they going to survive? She screamed hysterically. And worst of all, I was the last person who handled the money. We looked everywhere without any luck. And then, such a blessing, I saw Maya. I rushed to her: listen, I said, would you, by any chance, have seventy rubles? You know the odds were less than zero but why not to ask. And she said, "No, I don't have seventy rubles; I have only fifty-eight." Well, fifty-eight is better than nothing. Right? Grazina could justify losing twelve bucks but not the entire sum. So, I asked Maya if I could borrow from her and I promised her I would return the money as soon as I could. To tell you the truth I had no idea when and how I was going to do that because it was such a huge sum. But guess again — this morning I found those seventy rubles I couldn't find yesterday: Ha-ha-ha. I'd just misplaced them last night. So, here there are: fifty-eight rubles that I owe to Maya. Please give them to her and say thank you from me. Okay? She saved us."

Upon learning his story, I wasn't sure any more that Maya went to Moscow. So, on my way home I stopped at the public phone booth and made a call. She answered. I was right: she didn't go to Moscow; she just went downstairs to pick up the mail from her mailbox.

The sojourner

At the pulpit, called in Hebrew "bimah", a cantor hits the desk with his large and heavy palm, demanding everybody's attention and silence. It is time to chant the "Amida" prayer and it must be recited by each worshipper individually and mutely. The majority of the hanging in the back of the synagogue congregants decided to leave the building and have a smoke and a chat outside. Mikhail gets up to join the crowd. Todik, although not a smoker, follows our teacher and leaves us, me, Sergey and Nathan behind.

One of these five is a traitor. My enemy. Someone who was trying to put me into the GULAG. Someone who was trying to destroy my life. Who is that hideous man? Maya is not suspected. Only these five men, or one of them.

Who? Maybe Sergey? Well, naturally Sergey should be suspect number one. Only he and Maya were with me during the night when we read the novel. He obviously knows about its existence.

But do I have any indication, any evidence to think he was a culprit? Is he capable in general of doing such awful things? He is a serious person, responsible and tough. But is that enough to clear him of suspicion? Do I really know him that well?

Well, I certainly know several things about him. Not everything but some good, and bad, and unusual. Specific to him. For example I know that unlike most of us he didn't know that he was Jewish (actually, half-Jewish) until he turned sixteen.. The reason for such ignorance was quite simple: nobody informed him about this side of his ancestry.

Sergey was a child of a mixed marriage because only his father was a Jew. His mother was ethnic Russian. His family came to Lithuania from the city of Voskresensk, which is near Moscow. They came at the time when Sergey was still a little boy, maybe only two or three-years-old. In those days the Soviet authorities wanted to tame the nationalist mood of the indigenous Baltic population by trying to mix it with the people from the other parts of the Soviet Union. Therefore they encouraged native Russians and other ethnicities to move to the newly acquired Baltic states by offering them, as an inducement, better living conditions, higher salaries, and a more attractive environment. Lithuania still had a distinctive European charm, a unique atmosphere, totally absent in the inner parts of Russia. Sergey's parents were lured to Lithuania mainly by the prospect of getting their own one-bedroom apartment. In their native city of Voskresensk they didn't have a chance.

They settled in the suburb of Shanchiai in a depressing neighborhood of the multifamily buildings, textile factories and military installations, populated, for the most part, by the families of the "blue-color" workers and Red Army officers. All Sergey's friends and coevals were spawned from this tough "melting pot": it was a group of independent, hard-boiled, and vulgar guys, prone to indoctrination and deceit, eager to accuse someone else for their troubles and misfortune. And Sergey, just like most of his neighbors, saw the main cause of all injustices in the world in the presence of the annoying race of Jews — these abhorrent, greedy and deceitful creatures who used the blood of the Christian babies for their disgusting matzo bread and found a lot of fun in torturing pregnant Palestinian women. And just like most of his friends he laughed at the scornful anti-Semitic jokes, harassed his nerdy classmate Felix Sverdlov, drew swastikas on the briefcase of the school music teacher Isaac Abramovich Zingerman and vandalized gravestones in the old Jewish cemetery.

The change came when he was sixteen. He went to the government office to receive his ID, or an internal passport, which as well as other important biographical facts listed person's ethnicity.

The clerk who was supposed to issue the ID asked Sergey why he didn't write the truth in his application.

"What truth?" said a slightly puzzled Sergey, "Everything I wrote in my application is the truth."

"No, not at all. You stated, for example, that your father's ethnicity is Russian," said the clerk and his lips opened in a wide and cheerful smile.

"That is right," said Sergey, still bewildered.

"Wrong," said the clerk and his smile became even wider, "Didn't you look at your birth certificate? (And he hadn't) Your father is a Jew. And so you will be too if you won't state explicitly in your application that you want to have the ethnicity of your Russian mother."

It took some time for Sergey to absorb the news.

He laughed.

"This is a joke, isn't it?"

"A joke?" The clerk wasn't used to such insinuations.

"Ask your father," he said sternly, "or better still look at his passport."

Sergey didn't waste another second. He ran home eager to disprove the clerk's nasty lies.

A few days later he received his own passport. In the fifth line titled "the ethnicity" there was the shameful word "Jew". Just like a yellow star on the clothes of the ghetto dweller.

The transformation happened very quickly. He dropped out of high school and went to work as a machinist in a steel factory to avoid being financially dependent on his parents and after finishing the obligatory two years' military service became Mikhail's most dedicated, most devoted disciple.

Unfortunately, he could not dismiss his parents entirely. None of us could. The Soviet law demanded parents' consent as the necessary condition for applying for the exit visa.

"We do it for humanitarian reasons," explained Major Sidorchuk. "According to our communist morale children must support their parents. That is the rule, the rule of our socialist humanity. However, if parents officially reject and disown their child it means that they are willingly and lawfully refusing his or her help."

One day Sergey asked me and Maya to talk to his parents and try to persuade them to give him such permission. He himself didn't want to be present during this conversation and we never told him about its details.

His parents lived on the second floor in one of those numerous multifamily buildings, which, for their faceless and identical appearance, small rooms and non-existent sound protection, received the derogatory name "kruschevka".

The neighborhood — the street, as well as the houses on it — displayed the pinnacle of negligence and indifference: broken street lanterns, cracked, uneven walkways with the patches of old cobblestone pavement, stray haggard cats scavenging the overfilled garbage containers and the reek of urine from the filthy foyers. The whole this environment created a highly unappealing and disgusting atmosphere. Plus, according to the persistence among city residents' rumors, the neighborhood wasn't regarded as one of the safest, particularly after sunset, and we decided to call a cab on our way back.

The apartment itself, however, was neat and clean, it had a freshly painted floor, new wallpaper, and modern furniture.

There we met Sergey's parents: his mother, a weary looking middle-aged woman with silky gray hair and sleek agile body, still bearing a trace of her previous beauty, and his father, a short old man, bald and heavy, and most likely, much older than his wife. For the most part of our parley he sat quietly at the outer end of the table, occasionally injecting a word or two, and we instantly figured out who was the boss in the family.

"Sergey is our only child," commenced Sergey's mom, after we explained to her the purpose of our visit.

"He came quite late in our life," she continued, placing homemade chocolate cookies and a vase with the granulated sugar and teabags on the dinner table, "and he is very daring to us. Recently we had a difficult time socializing with him — he lives separately from us and doesn't come home too often... But he is still here, not too far from us, just a few blocks away. We still can help him if he needs."

During her speech, Sergey's dad turned on a small portable radio and placed it on the floor near the wall thus depriving his neighbors from the pleasure of gossiping and discussing the details of our conversation later on. Then he filled a big kettle with the water and put it on the gas stove.

"We know," sighed Sergey's mom after joining us at the table, "that our son wants to move to Israel. But we don't appreciate his idea. He is unprepared to live in a capitalist country, he is too young, too naïve, too vulnerable for that. Basically he is still a child. How is he going to survive in a country which is constantly at war and where every human behaves like a wolf to another human being?"

"This is a nonsense," Maya flared up, "communist propaganda. Who told you? Nobody is a wolf in Israel. You have been grossly misled."

"I don't know. I only repeat what they write in the newspapers. Why would they lie? Even if this is not the case, as you claim, the whole idea is too hard for us to swallow. Can't you see it? Do you understand that if he leaves, we will never see him again? Never. This is a one-way ticket. Our government doesn't allow the traitors to come back. It never does. No, no, we cannot let him go."

"But you can go together with him," I suggested, taking a generous bite from the chocolate cookie.

"We? Oh, no. That is impossible, young man. All our friends and relatives live here. Everybody. There is no one, not even a single creature who is waiting for us in Israel. Besides, we, my husband and I, were born here, in this country. I mean the Soviet Union. This is our birthplace, the place we are accustomed to, the place we have spent our entire lives. The Soviet Union is our homeland. Israel, on the other hand, is totally foreign to us: different culture, odd people, unfamiliar language, capitalism, oppression...we will never get used to it. It is totally, totally foreign to us... And what would we do there at our age anyway? We would never find a job and most likely will die from hunger and poverty. No, our relocation is out of question. Right, Boris?"

She turned to her husband for approval, and he nodded.

"But you are destroying Sergey's life, don't you understand it?" Maya flared up again. "Why are you thinking only about yourself? How about your son? Do you realize that he also has a life? He has many years in front of him. You cannot be so selfish! He wants to live in Israel."

I never saw Maya in such an assertive mood before. Something triggered her emotions.

"You are too immature, young lady, to teach us," retorted Sergey's mom, "we know what we are doing and what is good and what is bad for our Serezha."

"Oh, is that why he doesn't want to come here to stay with you? Don't you see that he is unhappy? Couldn't you sacrifice something for his sake?"

"Young lady, let me remind you one more time that we are much older than you are. We care about our son not less than you do..."

"No, you just want to show him how much power

you have. You want to show him that his fate depends on your good will. You act just like my dad does!"

"We don't know your dad, young lady. But if he cares about you the way we care about our son I can only applaud him."

"You, people, don't understand…"

"No, that is you — that is you who are too young to understand…"

"Ladies, ladies" interrupted Sergey's father, "let's try to be less emotional…"

His wife gave him such a ghastly look that he promptly shut his mouth.

For the next few minutes we sat quietly, numbed by the prospect of a new round of wrangles and spats, and only the portable radio on the floor still continued to play the mellowing melody of the first Chopin concerto.

But then the water in the kettle started to boil and the old man got up to remove it from the stove. He placed it on the iron stand in the middle of the table and served each one of us with the nicely decorated porcelain cup and plate.

"Well," said Sergey's mother, this time in a more conciliatory tone, "let us have some tea, young people. Let us put aside for now our disagreements. My sister from Moscow sent us recently a package with a real nice Ceylon blend. You won't be able to find such a thing over here."

"That is true," agreed Sergey's father, "Moscow

has a much better supply than we do. Even meat and milk products are more accessible there. If we would still be living in Voskresensk... It is much closer to Moscow..."

"We don't live in Voscresensk, Boris," his wife reminded him, "There is no reason to fantasize now."

Then she turned to us.

"We moved to Lithuania because we couldn't get an apartment back in Voskresensk. Do you understand? We wanted to have our own home, a small nest, a place where we could have a family and live in harmony and peace. That was our idea. We didn't ask for too much — did we? But look what's happened. Sergey, our only son, is gone, he hardly ever visits us. People outside our neighborhood are not friendly at all, they refuse to talk to us, they don't even answer if you ask them in Russian..."

"They want you to speak their language," I said.

"I would be glad to speak their language, but I don't know Lithuanian. What can I do? At my work, at home, with our friends ... we all speak Russian. Where would I learn it?"

"That doesn't bother them. The locals are convinced that since you are living in their country you must speak Lithuanian."

"Well, this is preposterous. We don't live in their country. We are all living in the Soviet Union and our common language here is Russian. Even more. I know for a fact that most of them actually can speak Russian much better than I can speak Lithuanian. But they refuse to do it because... because... it is just their chauvinism, their hatred toward anything not Lithuanian. That is right. You could hear left and right their slogan: Lithuania to Lithuanians!"

"I wouldn't call it chauvinism," I disagreed, "they feel that they live under the Russian yoke and they try to resist it by all possible means."

"I know some of them think that way. But that is nonsense. We don't oppress or occupy anybody. We all live in the family of nations and we are all equal here. And what would they do without our help anyway? Continue to be a third world country?"

And since none of us answered her, she proceeded further:

"It is tough for us here. We found that the locals have a totally different mentality and a different culture that's not even similar to ours. They are reserved and reticent people and constantly hiding their emotions. I would say they are not sincere. Not as open as we are."

And after a moment of silence she added calmly, "You were talking about moving to another country. Right? But look, we've had our experience already. We know what it is., It took us many, many years to adapt to the local customs and norms and yet we still don't feel fully comfortable here. Thanks to God, we are living in the Soviet Union. We can only imagine how it might be difficult and hard to move many thousand kilometers away, to start a new life, to start it from zero, from nothing, on the unfamiliar and most likely, unfriendly soil. What a nightmare! What a nightmare! Do you think we could wish something like this for our only child? When you get older and you have your own children, you'll start to understand us."

We didn't answer her. We were sitting, our lips close and tight and the tea was getting cold in the nice porcelain cups.

And then we left. Without any result.

Imagine how surprised we were when a week later Sergey informed us that his parents had agreed to disown him and to give him permission to apply for the exit visa. He was really happy.

And then came the day — the day of the departure, the day when he and his fictitious wife Maya Katz boarded the train carrying them toward their new homeland, toward Israel. Sergey's parents stood at a distance, afraid to come too close, fearful of getting into arguments and accusations at such a fateful moment. The day was sunny and warm, and the platform was crowded.. Sergey's friends played on the guitar, sang Israeli songs, drank wine, wishing departing folks good luck in their precarious endeavor, and there was a feeling as if an invisible fence had maliciously split this once happy and friendly family. But at the last moment, when the whistle from the locomotive ruptured the noise of the animated crowd, signaling thus the end of one life and the beginning of another, Sergey did something he didn't do for many-many years: he rushed toward his parents and hugged them very tightly, as tightly as he could.

And then he ran back toward the gaining speed train and jumped into the open door of the last carriage.

His mother stood strong. She didn't collapse in a frightful cry, not until the train made a turn and no one could see Sergey's grave face and his waving "goodbye" hand...

Parting forever, going to a strange land. These people didn't have even a hope to see each other ever again.

Sergey would be killed several years later, during the first Lebanon war, by a stray bullet. The rabbis wouldn't allow burying him in the Jewish cemetery because his mother wasn't Jewish and he would be laid outside the graveyard, by the fence, next to the thieves, child molesters and other criminals. Twelve thousand people would attend his funeral: his comrades from the army, his neighbors and co-workers and even people who had never met him when he was alive, all to pay respect to the soldier who sacrificed his life for theirs. Mikhail Rotman would hitchhike a car to come to this sad ceremony from the remote and uninhabited location to deliver a short but poignant speech. And Maya Katz, who wouldn't be Maya Katz any more but the honorable Baroness von Sheinkenfeld, would come in on her own private airplane from her estate in the Swiss Alps. She would bring Ilan, Sergey's only son, to show the boy his unfortunate father for the first and last time. Todik, Felix Sverdlov and even deformed and gray-haired Isaac Abramovich Zingerman, our former director of chorus, would all be present at this heartbreaking ceremony and only Sergey's elderly parents would be missing. The Soviet authorities wouldn't allow them to travel to Israel to attend the funeral of their only child. Why? I don't know. Perhaps Soviet bureaucrats were callous people, perhaps they do such things for political reasons, or perhaps they just wanted to make a point: you see, an orphan doesn't have parents, if he could live without them he definitely can die without them too.

This is how one person's short life ended. For a while Sergey's name, written on the simple bronze tablet, would still be visible to passing strangers and they might wonder why there were no stones on that plain and forsaken grave.

On the other hand, the story could be finished in a more positive tone. Let us hope that one day, Ilan, his son, will forgive his father's deficiencies and sins and will decorate the grave with a beautiful granite tombstone and Sergey will be granted after his death all those things he had missed during his lifetime.

Three thousand years ago, at Mount Sinai, Jewish co-travelers, bound by the same covenant, joined the unconventional tribe and through the centuries shared all its misfortunes and sufferings. Present day Jews are in part their descendants.

Similarly, not everyone who left Russia was a Jew: some had Jewish spouses; the others had Jewish fathers but not mothers; there were also those who had no connection to Judaism at all and they left Russia because they couldn't stand communism or were looking for a better life. They forged documents, paid hefty bribes to the Russian authorities and upon landing at Ben-Gurion airport became Israeli citizens under the Israeli law of return. According to the semi-official Israeli statistics at least one third of the newly arrived immigrants from the Soviet Union belonged to this diverse group of "non-real" Jews. What had happened to them after their arrival? Did they stay in their new home, or did they move on to the other places lured by the better opportunities and relief from the discontent, from their association with the strange tribe of people called Jews? Or did they, just like Sergey, fall in the battle defending the country which gave them a shelter at the time when they needed it?

Jewish communists

Amida is over and the smokers are coming back to the synagogue. They are bringing inside the pungent odor of decaying leaves and buoyancy of the cold fresh air. Todik talks eagerly to Mikhail, while Mikhail smiles in response. Apparently, this is one of Todik's customary jokes, the ones he usually picks up at his college dorm from his fellow-classmates. I could hear only the end of it, but everybody else laughs.

Everybody, except Sergey. He throws Todik a furious glance: "Now, this is not the time and place for such silly jokes."

Sergey is a serious man. A strong man. Could a person like him be a traitor, a snake, a scumbag?

I doubt it. But if not him, who could it be then? Only four of us were there, in the park, when Todik showed us his incredible "book". And if it wasn't me and it wasn't Sergey, and it wasn't Maya then it must be Todik himself. This is the only conclusion which follows from the logic.

But how could it be possible? Wasn't it Todik who actually showed us the "book" in the first place? Wasn't he the one about whom Lieutenant Belousov was making his enquiries?

Well, let's pretend that Todik disclosed to Lieutenant Belousov someone who returned the book to him but "forgot" to mention who gave it to him? Couldn't that be the case? What if he told Lieutenant Belousov only part of the truth, the part which is convenient for him?

Well, let us think methodically. The assumption I'd just made brings another important question: if this is indeed the case then who gave him the book? Who could be the person he is trying to protect? Todik didn't reveal to us where he got this "illegal material". Accidently or on purpose? I don't know. But one thing I know for sure, and it cannot be any other way: if my hypothesis is correct then the person he tries to protect, must be the one who knew Todik well enough to trust him.

And I started to sort out in my head all of Todik's acquaintances.

Mikhail's name came up first. But I instantly dismissed him. Not because he couldn't be a traitor (everybody could) (although it was extremely unlikely) but because he wouldn't give this book to Todik behind our backs. I knew this for sure. Most likely it would be all the way around.

Who is then left? Neither me nor Sergey nor Maya could be the person Todik would ever try to protect.

This leaves only Nathan.

Why him? Well, first of all, Nathan knows Todik for a much longer time than anybody else. They live next to each other and share the same backyard. And although Nathan is a year or two Todik's junior, nevertheless, during their childhood, they often played together because there were not too many mates of the similar age in the nearby vicinity. And then, what is more important, Nathan has the capability to possess things similar to the Uris novel *Exodus*.

Why? Well, because in Israel he has an uncle and he sends him barely legal items, like postcards of Israeli celebrities, *Life* magazines, musical records of the Barry sisters, the Beatles and others, all inappropriate for the Soviet citizens, stuff. Why couldn't they send him the *Exodus* as well?

Someone might be getting puzzled: how could Nathan get away with this audacity and still be out of prison? The answer to this question is simple: he has an aunt whose name is Mania.

Aunt Mania is a remarkable person. In one of the articles in the local communist daily *Tiesa* she was described as "the most esteemed member of the Lithuanian communist party, the pride and role model to the entire Lithuanian youth." If we could translate this incomprehensible description into a normal human language it would mean that she is an old-time hard-boiled communist, one of the individuals about whom you read in the papers but don't believe they actually exist. Several years ago, she, together with her husband Zygmas, occupied the highest positions in the local communist hierarchy: at one point she was the leader of the communist youth organization, then a government prosecutor and then a deputy controller.

The good times, however, went into obscurity. Zygmas, her husband, had passed away several years ago from an unexpected heart attack and one of the streets in the newest Vilnius neighborhood Zyrmunai was named in his honor. Aunt Mania herself, in the aftermath of the Arabs' defeat in the "Six-Day War", was relieved from all her duties and responsibilities and sent to "an honorable retirement", due to her unfortunate Jewish ancestry and a deplorable "Zionist" — her brother, an obscure Israeli communist, who was living in a remote kibbutz in the south of Israel. Nevertheless, despite all her misfortunes she was still able to retain many of her past privileges, and as a consequence, to continue to protect her relatives from the unrelenting KGB attention.

Bored by the involuntary departure and being childless, the aunt decided to concentrate all her excessive energy to foster communist morale and principles among her nieces and nephews. In fact, she is simultaneously a blessing and anathema for the Frenkel family. On the one hand they could enjoy a more comfortable life than any of us could even dream of but on the other she is the main reason why they are still living in the USSR.

"Only over my dead body," she was saying not once, "that Abram and Nathan will become cannon fodder for the Israeli oppressors and colonizers."

In vain, Nathan's parents tried to persuade Aunt Mania to change her mind and allow them to immigrate to Israel. In Israel, they were saying, Abram and Nathan might become members of the communist party, just like Mania's own brother, the one who lives in kibbutz. But all their arguments fell on deaf ears because Aunt Mania maintained an unwavering belief that all communists outside Soviet Union are either misguided liberals or lackeys of American imperialism.

"We, Soviet communists," she kept saying," have two kinds of enemies: open and veiled. The open enemies are capitalists, imperialists, German revanchists and Zionists while the veiled ones are those devious turncoats who pretend to be socialists and progressives, just like we are, but in reality promote bourgeois ideology and values. Out of the two the second kind is by far more dangerous because these phony progressives are trying to conceal their true anti-revolutionary identity and thus mislead the public. Therefore, we set up a fight against them as a priority in our struggle for a better future."

When occasionally I visit Nathan and see in his house this slim and petite sixty something years old lady with her pleasant smile, fast moves and graceful gestures, I have a real difficulty to imagine how such a delicate creature could be so cruel and merciless during her turbulent past. Nathan told me several fascinating stories about her exploits during World

War Two; how she, for example, with great risk to her life, infiltrated a Polish "Land Army" detachment to obtain information regarding upcoming Warsaw resurrection or how she, as a member of the communist guerilla group "for the Motherland" in Rudniki forest, was executing in cold blood captured German officers and soldiers. Due to her short height, they had to kneel in front of her, so it would be convenient for Aunt Mania to put her handgun into their open mouths.

"It didn't give me any pleasure to execute those filthy fascists," she was explaining to her nephew, "quite the opposite. But on the other hand, I had no pity for them either. It was not too different than squashing a cockroach or killing a mosquito. Some of the prisoners died with dignity but there were others, spineless and fainthearted who begged me for mercy. Some even tried to kiss and lick my boots. These were especially disgusting. But despite that I despised about them I was trying to encourage these pitiful fascists to face a death like a man. You were brave enough to come here, on our land, I was telling them, to murder innocent people. Now be brave enough to pay for your crimes.

"And to tell you the truth, my dear nephew, we had no other choice, anyway, even if we would have any desire to spare their useless lives. We could not take them with us into the woods for we didn't have enough food even for ourselves. Besides, we were constantly on the run, chased by their fascist comrades. We also could not let these bastards go free because they would once again take the guns and come back and try to kill us. It was a war: either we kill them, or they will kill us. We favored the first outcome."

She was seventeen when she was arrested for the first time.

Lithuania was then going through a period of peculiar development. Although nominally a republic with a duly elected and functional parliament, she, in reality, was ruled by the military junta, headed by the "president for life" dictator Smetona. And while the newly formed state experienced the upsurge of the national revival and unprecedented economic growth, many democratic institutions were absent, banned or suppressed. Among all the parties in the country only one, "Nationalist", was legitimate, all others were prohibited, freedom of press was severely limited and trade unions were non-existent. This strange situation particularly appeared to be in the Jewish community.

Aunt Mania, as one of the members of that community, found her answer by joining the ranks of then illegal communist party.

"Jews represented the most disadvantageous part of the population," she was explaining to us time and again, "but we, Jewish communists, didn't concentrate on our own matters, like, let's say, Bund and other, so-called, socialists did. No, we were internationalists and struggled for the rights and freedom of all people: of

Jews, Lithuanians, Russians... We wanted everybody to be equally happy and we didn't separate people according to their religion, ethnicity or nationality. For us there were just two categories of human beings: hard working proletarians and capitalist exploiters, oppressors and oppressed."

"I will give you just one example of the unfairness we faced during the times of Smetona's dictatorship," she continued. 'One day, a stranger by the name of Peresman came to Linkuva, the town where I was born. He was a real Jewish capitalist — an unscrupulous and very greedy man. Our town didn't have electricity then. So, he bought an old, dilapidated barn and built an electrical generator inside it. Then he put poles across the town, ran wires between them and began to supply electricity to everyone who was willing to pay for it. As I said, he was a stingy person and did everything himself: putting light bulbs in the houses, writing the bills and collecting the money. When he got rich enough, he hired Dovid-der-Shlosser, one of our fellow-workers, to do the dirty jobs for him while paying this poor man pennies. The price for the electricity though was astronomical — only a small number of residents could afford it. We asked that bastard-capitalist more than once to listen to us. We said to him, "Comrade Peresman, electricity is a necessity, not a luxury, everybody needs it, not just rich people so could you, please reduce your draconian fees? Do you know what his answer was? I cannot do it because in such a case I won't make any profit."

"Money was everything to him. But when we, the communists took control in 1940 and established our own democratic laws, we nationalized his electrical power station. Don't get me wrong — we were very generous to Mr Peresman and we gave him a position of director in this power plant and a very good salary. Do you want to know how he responded to our generosity? He set a fire and burned down the barn together with the generator. The court sentenced him to twenty-five years of hard labor in a Siberian labor camp. I was then a prosecutor and asked for the death penalty. Why? Because he destroyed not a private but a government property and deprived poor folks of the town of their essential utility. That is why. Unfortunately, the judge was too lenient. No wonder: a year later the judge himself was found guilty of the crimes he committed against our socialist state and he was also sent to the labor camp together with his whole family. Well, we sent his family actually just to exile."

"His family? Did they also do some nasty crimes?" asked Nathan.

"Not exactly. But we didn't want to separate families — it would be too cruel for their children. Besides, they were relatives of the extremely dangerous criminal and presented a potential threat to our society. It was done, my dear nephew for everyone's good to prevent what is called "the circle of violence" on the part of criminals.

"But isn't it unfair to punish a person for a crime he didn't actually commit?"

"You need to understand — it was not a punishment; it was a prevention. And it was done, let me repeat, for a common good."

"Even for a common good..."

"Yes, my dear, for a common good. You are too young to understand. The authority has the right to impose strict rules and laws on individuals for the sake of the welfare of the majority. It happens all the time. Take, for example, the present law, which requires you to wear a car seatbelt. Or, let's say, when a government imposes a quarantine on a certain part of the population to prevent the spread of infectious disease. Are the people who are locked inside their homes guilty of something? No. They might not be even ill. Then, why are they kept like criminals in prisons? For a common good, my dear, for a common good: to protect other people from getting sick. We also were trying to prevent the spread of the disease, although a disease of a different kind. Actually, it was the deadliest disease of all. It was called "a brown plague". Have you heard such an expression? A brown plague. It was a fascism. We needed to stop it. And remember — a common good should always take priority over individuals. Always. Even in our partisan group in Rudniki forest during the war we had certain cases. One of our fighters, for example, refused to wear a helmet, claiming that it was too heavy, inconvenient for him, and so on. We tried to persuade the silly fellow that it was necessary to wear it, but he stubbornly argued that we had no right to tell him what he should or shouldn't wear. That was intolerable. And what was even more important: he showed the disobedience. I had no reason to explain to him or to anyone else why I ordered this or that: all partisans of our detachment had to obey my orders without questioning them. So, to make the long story short, we had to execute the insolent fellow in front of the other fighters to make a good lesson for everybody."

We listened to her with open mouths.

'Don't compare, young men, the peaceful times to a war," she said, noticing the expressions of our faces, "Unfortunately, we had to enforce obedience in such a tough way. "

"For such small things!" couldn't hold Nathan.

"There are no small things when you are fighting at war. Everything is important. And particularly strict discipline — this is not just important, it is critical: it is the key for survival and ultimate victory. You probably heard about Jews who, during Holocaust, went like sheep to the slaughter. Nazis and their Lithuanian lackeys were lining these pitiful Jews at the edge of the pit and shooting them at will. And no one lifted a hand to resist the slaughter. No one. Do you know why? I heard anti-Semitic insinuations claiming that Jews were cowards. It is not true. Jews acted this way not because they were cowards but because they didn't have a leader; they didn't have a man who could unite a bunch of diverse and separate individuals into one unified team and lead it to the victory by the iron will of his character, by the strong discipline and his unchallenged authority. When such a leader could be found, like during the famous escape from the concentration camp of Sobibor (I am talking about Soviet army officer Pechorsky), Jews didn't act any differently than anybody else."

"Or like Moses, when he led the Jews out of Egypt," said Nathan.

Aunt Mania lifted her eyebrows.

"You should be ashamed of yourself," she said, "to believe in such things. Who is that Moses? A mythical figure, a fictional character, created by the fantasy of the uneducated peasants. These fabricated fairy tales are only good for the kindergarten students. Capitalists employ them to deceive naïve people. I am talking about real men, Nathan. Real. About comrade Stalin, for example. Nowadays many people blame him for some injustice he committed during those turbulent days. But without him and his strong leadership we probably wouldn't ever have achieved our victory in the war against the Nazis, a great victory which liberated not just us but the whole of Europe and Lithuania would never have become a socialist country. I know; you, the young generation, don't appreciate our past efforts. It happens because you, guys, don't even know how cruel life is in capitalist countries. We felt it on our own skins and in our stomachs when we lived in the "banana republic" of Lithuania under the brutal rule of the military junta and its secret police."

"But I heard from my Lithuanian friends," I timidly objected to her statement, "that Soviet NKVD was much more brutal than Lithuanian secret police. Just before the war it deported many thousands of Lithuanians to Siberian labor camps."

"Nonsense," responded Aunt Mania, "your friends, young man, are probably listening to the rightfully banned Voice of America. This station says nothing but propaganda. In August of 1940, when the democratically-elected Lithuanian parliament expressed the desire of the Lithuanian people to join the Soviet Union, NKVD indeed conducted some arrests, I admit it. It had to clean the country from the undesirable elements, such as Trotskyists, nationalists, capitalists, radical religious clerics of all kinds— Jewish, Polish, Lithuanians, from people's enemies, in other words, for the sake of the rest of the population, the progressive part of it, to allow it to enjoy a happy and meaningful life. All the convicted criminals received a fair trial, by the way, trust me. I, myself, prosecuted several of these scoundrels including the notorious Jewish fascist Menachem Begin. Unfortunately, he survived the labor camp and became lately a high-ranking chieftain in Israel. Just like another villain — his buddy, one-eyed Moshe Dayan.

It is also true, that sometimes, for a common good, we had to deport the entire families of those despicable bandits. But it was done for their own good, young man. Take, for example, the families of the deported Jewish capitalists: they all survived the war unlike their relatives who remained in Lithuania."

(But I was talking about different times, Aunt Mania. Almost a year later, in June, 1941, just before the start of the war, NKVD conducted a succession of mass arrests. This time, unlike previously, it wasn't Jews, Poles, or Russians who were the victims, but only ethnic Lithuanians. And according to several historians, more than forty thousand people, often entire families, without any trial, were put on freight trains and deported to the desolate parts of Siberia and then released there without any means of survival.

Later Jews would be blamed for their mistreatment — just like they are blamed for everything else.

And the crowds of the furious mob would go on a rampage to punish the awful killers of Jesus, NKVD operatives and soulless usurers, capitalists and Bolsheviks, atheists and religious clericals, Zionists, nationalists and cosmopolites, the permanent cause of everything what is bad on the earth.)

One of the most infamous killings occurred in Lietukis garage in the center of Kaunas on June 25 and 26 of 1941. It took place during broad daylight and was captured on camera by a private in the

German army Wilhelm Gunsilius:

There are contradictory accounts to what had happened here, as many variants as there are witnesses. The most plausible and reliable sequence of events, however, could be summarized as follows.

On 25 June, in the afternoon, a group of NKVD operatives (apparently some Jews, but some non-Jews also) arrived at the garage with the aim of seizing a car or a truck and escaping on it from the city. Either they tried to use force to achieve their goal or one of the mechanics in the garage recognized among them his former investigator and torturer, but the whole group was arrested, interrogated and after a short trial put to death. Meanwhile other insurgents, who probably heard the rumors about this makeshift court, began to bring in more and more suspected "chekists". Among them probably were some random Jews as well, who accidently happened to be at the wrong time in the wrong place.

The beatings and murders continued in broad daylight for a couple of days.

Some historians identified the young man in the picture as Juozas Luksha, one of the most prominent Lithuanian fighters in the struggle for its independence after World War Two. He was killed in 1951 in the ambush with the elite KGB unit and became a Lithuanian national hero.

Unfortunately, this photo was not available in the Soviet Union (Soviet authorities tried to diminish the extent of the Lithuanian participation in the murders and therefore sought to hide any material which could contradict their official narrative) because Aunt Mania mentioned his name several times and I missed the opportunity to ask her more about it.

"In June of 1941 I was a prosecutor at the trial of one of the most notorious bandits, Juozas Luksha," she told us once. "He was a senior member of the criminal gang called "Lithuanian Activists Front" and also the leader of the students' cell in Kaunas University. During his interrogation I had several heated debates with that fascist. Despite being a murderer and criminal, he was also an eloquent person, skillful in presenting arguments and logical conclusions and it was a great pleasure for me to foil all his vile tricks.

"You, Jews, he was saying, have been living in

our country for many years. In all this time we treated you reasonably well, considering the magnitude of the annoyance you have caused to us by your strange customs and behavior. Our great king Vytautas permitted you to come and settle here, in our land, when crusaders and mobs in Western Europe were murdering and torturing your ancestors. He provided you guys with the shelter and safety and allowed you to practice your rituals and religion. You prospered; you became richer than we are. But instead of being thankful for all the good deeds that we did to you; you decided to become Russian lackeys and join our tormentors and oppressors. Apparently, it was not even enough for you, Jews, to impose on us your shameful usury. Your Jewish commissars and NKVD operatives moved even further — now they are persecuting and torturing our people, the true natives of this land, in the most despicable and heinous way: they are sending whole families to Siberia, to hard labor and slavery. Is that how you, Jews, are paying back for our hospitality? But be aware: those who plant injustice will harvest it…"

"Don't try to scare me," I said to the bastard, "you shouldn't forget who is on trial — you or me? In our new socialist homeland there are no more guests and no more owners, no slaves and no masters; all people here are equal. Remember that. We all are the same people living under the same sun. And we are not sending certain individuals to the labor camps to make slaves from them. No, we do it in the hope that hard work will transform these misguided folks to become useful members of the new and progressive society. I also can assure you, that we will never tolerate the racist sentiments and lies of yours. First of all, this is not true; not only are Jews commissars and NKVD operatives. Quite few of the NKVD workers are actually your folks — the honest and righteous ethnic Lithuanians..."

(Here I must interrupt Aunt Mania's revelations. What was the Soviet's business getting involved in the life of the small nation? People lived in their own country, good or bad, nationalists, capitalists, workers and peasants. They didn't harm anybody and didn't want to harm; absorbed in their own matters they had no intention of becoming involved in Soviet internal affairs. Why then did the USSR government get an impression that it had the right to do the opposite?

I know Aunt Mania's answer: Soviet communists cared about all people in the world, sometimes even more than they care about their own relatives and siblings. They wanted to see everybody as a happy family of equal nations and therefore they stretched out their arms to help uninformed Lithuanians to achieve this precious goal, even if the Lithuanians themselves never asked for such help. It must be then just a simple human compassion when in the summer of 1940 they flooded the conquered nation with NKVD operatives, with those whose task was to chase down all the real and imaginary enemies of the new regime.)

"As an unrepentant and hardened criminal this fascist Luksha was sentenced to death," Aunt Mania continued, "our judges rightfully concluded that hard labor would not be enough to transform him into a decent human being. However, due to the fast advance of the German army in the summer of 1941, he temporarily evaded his punishment. His buddies from the criminal LAF organization released him from the "yellow" prison in Kaunas on the second day of the war and later he joined the Nazi administration and participated in killings of the civilian population. After 1945 he became the leader of one of those vicious bands called "forest brothers" which terrorized peaceful peasants and our sympathizers. Eventually, the soldiers of the Red Army caught and killed him in an ambush and justice finally was achieved."

"Did many local Lithuanians participate in mass murders?" asked Nathan curiously.

"Yah, there were a few of them just like this scumbag, Luksha. But there were also Lithuanians who saved Jews. Quite a few, in fact. I personally know several of them. Great people. They saved Jews by risking their own lives. And not only theirs. To make their death more painful the Nazis first were killing members of their families, before killing the perpetrators themselves."

"The perpetrators?'

"Of course the perpetrators. According to the

Nazis' fascist laws to be a Jew was a crime. To save a Jew was also a crime. Therefore law-abiding citizens didn't save Jews. Only lawbreakers did. Later these people were called righteous among righteous. They were the real heroes, these ordinary Lithuanians — devotees to the principles of international solidarity."

"Maybe they did it because they felt themselves as true Christians?"

"Nonsense. Christianity, as any religion, is extremely reactionary and inhuman. Karl Marx once correctly said: the religion is the opiate for the masses. No, their actions had nothing to do with the religion. Quite the opposite. You may not know but many local priests helped Nazis to commit these horrible crimes. You should read my book, my memoirs: I explained everything there. And if you will have questions I will be happy to answer them. I never run away from the questions because I know I am right."

It was only partly true. Indeed, she didn't mind arguing with us unless there was a question she couldn't find the answer to.

"I think," she often used to say, "that everyone is entitled to have his or her opinion. This is normal; this is all human. And it is also incredibly challenging when someone disagrees with you. You must overcome your opponent's arguments and beat him in a fair and logical way. This is a lot of fun. That is how life is supposed to be. Don't you think so? I'll tell you even more — if everybody agreed with everyone on everything, life would be extremely boring. I never minded arguing with anybody. And I still don't mind it. I may have a look of a sixty-year-old woman but in my heart, I am still seventeen. And when I was seventeen, we used to argue all the time. All the time. Days and nights. It was such a wonderful time! We argued about everything — about politics, science, books, and new movies... I see sometimes how you children, entertain yourselves nowadays — by drinking hard liquor and singing the disgusting anti-Soviet songs of that lousy bard Vysotsky, but I can tell you: there is nothing more entertaining than having arguments and discussions. (Aunt Mania probably never heard about the restaurant "Coffee and Ice cream"). Efforts to discover the truth... And the great joy when you do it. We were the lucky people then..."

I cannot imagine what kind of luck she had spending the best years of her life in filthy prison cells or in the freezing dugouts in the Rudniki forest, living under the constant threat of being arrested and killed.

"Do you know what my dream was then?" she asked us once, "I dreamt that one day I may get out after my dinner without finishing it, that I could leave some food on the table and say to myself — I've had enough, I don't want any more. That was my dream".

"We fought, we sacrificed our lives that the future generations won't have such dreams," she said, "we worked very hard to achieve our goal, to create a wonderful place of social justice and universal brotherhood. Yes, we made a few mistakes during our long-lasting struggle but who doesn't? My late husband Yurgis was an intelligent man (Why, do you think, I married him?) and he used to say, 'Both smart people and stupid make mistakes. The difference is that smart people don't repeat them.' "He was a great man — compassionate, strong and tender, not just clever. His parents, devoted Catholics, fervently opposed our relationship. But he disobeyed their wishes and married me. And we lived together many wonderful years. Unfortunately, we didn't have our own children. But we saw you guys, the new generation, as our adopted children, deserved to be living in a better place and a better life. We struggled a lot to achieve it and despite all the ups and downs, we finally reached our objective, and you are living now in the country which provides the best conditions for all humans: you have free education and free health care, there is no unemployment in our country and no homelessness; everybody has food and a roof above his or her head. You don't need to worry about the next day: the government will take care of all your needs..."

"But don't you think these are the same conditions under which convicts live in prisons?' asked her Mikhail.

He was passing by after visiting Nathan's older brother Abram and stopped for a moment in the living room to say "hello."

"They also have free medical care and free education," Mikhail continued, ignoring Aunt Mania's attempt to object, "and the roof above their head, and plenty of food, and they also don't worry about the next day for they know for sure that prison administration will take care of all their needs. Just like citizens of our country they don't feel responsibility for anything in the jail. Nevertheless, all of them, all the prisoners, for some reason, want to get out, as far as they could, away from this place of "common equality" and "social justice…""

"I keep wondering, young man," finally, Aunt Mania was able to interrupt our teacher, "why you didn't join the company of those criminals yet? It gives you just another proof of how tolerant our government is. In the West you would be jailed for such comparison in no time, just like it was in Lithuania during the Smetona dictatorship. You don't know and therefore you don't realize how lucky you are living here, in the USSR, and not in the colonial outpost of the American imperialism by the name of Israel."

"Israel is our ancient homeland. Until its establishment we all lived in exile, in galut, relying on the good will of our hosts. Some Jews kept forgetting that simple fact until the local population reminded them once in a while. Indeed there are people who need a whip to start to learn. "

"And move to Palestine?"

"To Israel"

"To oppress the native population? Tell me then, what rights did Jews have to settle on the land which belongs to somebody else? Did you ever try to answer such a question, young man?"

"If you mean Palestinians then the land doesn't belong to them. And never did."

"You say nonsense, young man. These people lived on that land for many centuries. They are indigenous to the country, they are aborigines".

"It is absolutely irrelevant who are aborigines and who are not because living on a certain piece of land doesn't entitle anybody to own it. These are two completely different notions. Our friend Sergey, for example, also lives in the apartment. So, what? It doesn't belong to him; it belongs to his landlord. Your apartment doesn't belong to you also; it belongs to the Soviet government. You don't own it. Palestinians also never owned the land they have been living on. There were other owners: Jews, Romans, Crusaders, Ottomans, Brits… Never Palestinians. Jews settled on that land more than three thousand years ago when they escaped from Egyptian slavery."

"This is a myth, young man. Pure myth. There is not even one single piece of evidence in the Egyptian records that an exodus from Egypt ever took place. I also read the books."

"No, there is. The narrative of Egyptian historian Manetho . He claims that an Egyptian priest by the name of Osarseph became the leader of the lepers and other "unclean" and oppressed people and led them out of Egypt. Osarseph later took another name for himself — Moses. It is all in Manetho's manuscript. The story is different than in the Bible, I admit it, but it would be ridiculous to expect from the Egyptian sources to hear Jewish narrative. Jews then settled in the Holy Land and that is where the Jewish nation was born, where Jews became Jews. And just like any individual has the right to live in the place he was born, so does the nation."

"There is no such thing as a Jewish nation, young man. Have you ever read the excellent book of Yevgenii Yevseev, *Fascism under the Blue Star*? Read it. I strongly recommend it to you. The author is a prominent member of our communist party, has a Ph.D. in history and he is professor of sociology at Minsk University. In his book he proves that Jews lack all the attributes which are necessary for a group of people to form a nation and therefore they cannot be a nation. They are just the adherents of Judaism — the most reactionary religion of all world religions. Why? Because it gave birth to the infamous ideology of Zionism, the political forerunner of other hideous ideologies like fascism and Nazism. Yevseev gives undeniable evidence of the shameful collaboration between Zionists and Nazis during World War Two. He also explains why such a prominent Nazi ideologist like Dr Mandelbrod stated not once that Nazis took their ideas directly from the book *Rome and Jerusalem* written by the first world Zionist, Moses Hess. The notions of the "superior race" and "chosen people", the legitimacy of the seizure of other people's land and the criminal methods to attain it — they all came from the Jewish Talmud. These ideas established the base for the evil Zionist ideology and were first practiced by Zhabotinsky and his followers, like that racist rabbi from New York... What's his name...? Eh...eh... Meir Kahane...

"Meir Kahane is a hero," interrupted Mikhail, "he is helping us more than anybody else to get out of the Soviet Union".

"Shame on you, young man. Meir Kahane is a Nazi, even worse than Hitler was. Racists like him use and are still using the Talmud to promote the ideas of the superior race, the same ideas which led in the past to the creation of concentration camps and subsequent mass murders."

"So, what was bad — the notion of the superior race or the creation of the concentration camps?" asked Mikhail.

"Both. There is no difference between them. One obviously leads to another."

"Indeed? In such a case what led the Bolsheviks to establish concentration camps in Siberia? Also Talmud?"

"You have been intensely brainwashed, young man, by the illegal western radio stations. Our camps are reeducation facilities for the convicted criminals.

Criminals, young man, are convicted by our system of justice, the most objective system in the world. That is it. I don't want to argue with you any more."

This was the old and well known to us Aunt's Mania's "song". While she never objected to dispute and disagree, the moment she ran out of arguments she simply would end the conversation and walk away. Just like that. As if nothing had happened. Long time ago we have concluded that it was impossible to change her mind, to convince her in anything that would contradict the beliefs she had acquired during her adolescent years. It would be just a waste of anyone's efforts. All her relatives had already tried to explore their talents of persuasion and all of them, without any exception, had failed. She continued to remain unwavering in her belief that socialism and communism are the best political systems in the world.

But several years later, however, the universe, in accordance with Hegel's philosophical insights, negated the negation and Lithuania once again became an independent state. It abandoned its previous socialist system, restored capitalism and disillusioned Aunt Mania immigrated to Israel. The new Lithuanian government didn't treat her as well, with the same kind of respect she enjoyed during the previous administration: it took away the big portion of her hefty pension, her unhindered power and many other privileges. The street which carried the name of her late husband Yurgis was renamed and became "Yozas

Luksha" street. Everything in Lithuania has turned upside down: those who in the past were "partisans" became "bandits" and those who were "bandits" became "partisans". A new government persecutor, inadvertently a distant relative of the same Yozas Luksha, has initiated a court procedure to indict Aunt Mania on charges of war crimes and crimes against Lithuanian people. She didn't take all these measures as easily as she did at the time of her youth and soon left the place she promised never to leave.

Israel reinstated her pension and gave her other retirement benefits (although she didn't work in Israel even for one day and never paid any taxes), like free health care and a hefty "immigrant package". It also put pressure on the Lithuanian government to drop all the charges against her. She was honored by the highest Israeli officials for her role in the fight against the Nazis on Lithuanian soil and every year during the annual veterans' parade, in commemoration of the victory over Nazi Germany, she was walking in the first row proudly displaying on her chest many Soviet medals. In rare interviews to the progressive media reporters she, nevertheless, continued to bash Israel for the alleged imperialism, colonialism, and violations of human rights, exactly as she did back in communist Lithuania.

Nathan became an officer in the Israeli Defense Forces, the notorious "cannon fodder" while his older brother Abram completed the retraining, got a degree in computer science and moved with his family to one of the Israeli settlements on the West Bank where he befriended David Axelrod, a great-grandson of another fighter against Zionism, Leon Trotsky.

Modern days Joseph

The evening service is coming to its end. The majority of the congregants who spent their time in the rear part of the synagogue had already left the building and went home to have a late dinner. Those who sit in the front are still here. "Frume idn" as Mikhail calls them. Most likely they will be fasting until tomorrow night. I promised Mikhail that I will join them. Now I wonder if I will be able to hold up for so long; I had never tried it before.

I am curious who also will fast. I think Sergey and Maya definitely will. Mikhail maybe.. I am not sure, however, about Todik. He doesn't take religion too seriously; constantly mocks Sergey's devotion and makes silly jokes about pious congregants. I really don't understand what brings him here. Even now it looks like he is quite tired and eager to go home. And it seems that just out of the boredom he decided to provoke Sergey to go back into the debate they had yesterday during our Hebrew class.

During that lesson Mikhail told us the story about Joseph and his brothers and asked us to repeat it in Hebrew. However, it did not work that way: instead, we began to argue in Russian, everyone rushing to express a view on the subject. And although we mostly agreed that nowadays, in the similar situation, people would act in a similar way, when it came to the discussion of the pharaoh's dream about seven cows our opinions had split, and the excitement went overboard.

"I cannot believe it," said Todik, "it is nonsense. The pharaoh couldn't give Joseph so much power, based solely on the interpretation of his dream. I wish I could find someone as stupid as this pharaoh. What if Joseph was wrong? Did this kind of thought ever cross his stupid mind? But even if Joseph, let's say, was right — even in such a case the decision to elevate the former slave and prisoner to such a high position and give him so much power and responsibilities is beyond any rationale. I don't believe the whole story."

"Why not?" retorted Sergey, "there are situations when a certain person exhibits so much confidence that everybody begins to trust his infallible abilities. This was, probably, one of such rare instances."

"Is that so? How do you know?"

"Do you remember the story? These were the priests in pharaoh's court who suggested to pharaoh to appoint Joseph to the position of the caretaker. Obviously, they all were impressed by his abilities to interpret dreams."

"Maybe they were but I wasn't. If I would be in place of pharaoh, I would never allow Joseph to take care of the government business. The man just got out of prison!"

"These were different times, Todik," interrupted Mikhail, "prior to GULAGs and KGB..."

His remark, however, couldn't stop them from arguing.

They continued to argue even after we left Mikhail's apartment and went outside and even when I said "good bye" to them on the corner of Kestchio and Gedimino streets. And now it seems as if they started it all over again.

I can understand Pimple's impatience: the service indeed had lasted for too long already. More than two hours. Thank God — I wasn't hungry.

The thoughts of a juicy steak in a savory mushroom sauce with a glass of cold beer don't bother me yet. Perhaps they will come tomorrow, during afternoon classes in my engineering school in which case I will probably skip the lectures and come here, to be among people with a similar mindset for I bet by then they all will be thinking about a juicy and yummy steak.

So, it is a done deal. I can use my occupation as a student to my advantage. I am the lucky one because not everyone in the Soviet Union has an opportunity to attend the service before the sunset. Despite the loudly declared freedom of religion Soviet law forbids working folks to take a day off during their religious holidays. Therefore they can come only when they are able to come. It is called "a separation of church and state".

Suddenly a lame man, who usually directs the sequence of the proceedings (although, as a rule, only after a long and noisy dispute with the other members of the congregation) Chaim Tsypkin announces that the time has come for the "mourner Kaddish" — the last prayer of the evening. Several congregants rise from their seats. These are the ones who lost members of their families during the last year or those, who commemorate the anniversary of their deaths on this specific day. Chaim Tsypkin also rises from the bench together with the others. In truth, he doesn't really know the exact day his parents were murdered but decided to observe it on the day of Yom Kippur, during the holiest time of the year.

"It seemed to me like the most appropriate way to do it," he explained to me once, during our Shabbos "Kiddush" dinner, after we consumed a good amount of jolly substance and were in a mood to speak casually and freely.

"My family and I became separated when the Nazis were liquidating the small ghetto, which was on another side of Raudondvario Plentas street," he said to me, "There was a Nazi officer by the name of Helmut Rauca who conducted the selection. He separated me from my family. My mom was on her knees begging him not to do it but the evil man just pointed with his finger in the direction of the crowd destined to be executed. He didn't utter one word. That was particularly painful for me because I did a lot of work for him, but he couldn't do just this small favor for us."

"What kind of work did you do for him?"

"Plumbing."

"Plumbing? Are you a plumber?"

"I used to be. I know it sounds weird — Jewish plumber. But I wasn't really a plumber. I was an installator. Do you know the difference between "installiator" and a regular plumber? Chaimke-der-installator — that is how everybody called me then. We lived in Slobodke not far from the place where the veterinary academia is now. I was about fourteen when the brothers Kurlyandchik installed water pipes on our street. It was amazing a miracle when the water began to flow. I couldn't believe that each house might have its own private faucet. We all collected water then from the water well down the street. I was so impressed that on the same day I told my parents, I wanted to be an installator. They obviously didn't appreciate my choice. My mother nearly had a heart attack. But then my father said, "Every flock has a black sheep. So, let Chaimke be ours.""

"He probably wanted you to become a famous violin virtuoso. All Jewish parents do."

"Who? My father? Oh, no, he wasn't that type of a dreamer. He wanted me to take over our family business."

"What business?"

"We had a small grocery shop: a parnose of sorts — the source of our income. Well — it wasn't really an income. I remember, once, in the Thirties, the famous Zionist Zeev Zhabotinsky visited our city. He gave a lecture in the local "Maccabee" club on Daukanto street. He said, "Jews of Kovno, if you want to survive — immediately go to Palestine. Soon Hitler will come to your city and he will take from you everything you have: your businesses, your houses and even your lives". My father came home from the lecture and said, "Why would Hitler need our shop? What good could he get from it? It gives nothing but tsores. Our shop cannot feed even ourselves." In other words: Zhabotinsky didn't convince my father. And what do you think? Instead of Hitler came Russians and our business began to boom — in one week the officers of the Red Army purchased in our store more stuff than we could ever sell in a whole year. They emptied all our closets. Completely. But my father wasn't happy: he couldn't replenish the goods. And the brothers Kurlyandchik were also not happy. Not every Jew was happy. Only our local communists walked like they'd won a lottery ticket. Well, for me the new authority was not too bad also. Why? Because everybody needs water. I had a very good profession. No doubt; it saved me during World War Two."

"Do you mean — you were treated better than others by the Nazis?"

"Better? Oh, no. Only if I did the job to Rauca's

satisfaction. I was treated like everybody else. However, this happened quite rarely. Most of the time he was unhappy with my work. In such instances he whipped me with the leather belt. The amount of lashes each time was different and depended on his mood. I had to lie down on my stomach with my pants down and loudly count those lashes and after each one of them to scream, "This is the correct punishment for my lousy job."

"Then how did the plumbing help you to survive? I don't understand."

"That is simple. I will tell you." Chaim grabbed a half-emptied bottle of 100 proof "Maluninku" liquor and filled his and my glasses, "Nu, L'Chaim! For your and my heath!"

And then he emptied his glass in a one long gulp.

"These Nazis were not stupid," he continued, after wiping his lips with the back of the palm. "They were Germans. Germans, you know, are prudent and meticulous people. First of all, they got rid of the useless folks like old pensioners, intelligentsia, all sorts of poets, rabbis... Why? Why would the Nazis need them? Think for yourself. How could a drunken hoodlum with a gun in his hand benefit from the knowledge of ancient Greek philosophy, or calculus or passages from Talmud? Answer me. These scholars were doomed. The Nazis didn't need them and therefore they were the first to go. Next came the turn of the young and strong fellows. But we, the barbers, shoemakers, carpenters, and plumbers, we were the last ones on that line. For Germans we were the most important people in the ghetto. Farshteistu? That is the reason why many of us have survived."

He filled our glasses again:

"L'Chaim, my friend! Tsu gezunt!"

I am thrilled to be treated like that, like an equal, like another adult. It is, actually, the main reason I was attending these Shabbos services once in a while.

It started a couple years ago when I was still a high school student. One Saturday morning I was walking along Ozeskenes street, heading toward my classmate Kolya Ivanov's apartment. Suddenly short lame man, appeared in front of me, blocking my way.

Why did I need to visit Kolya at such an early hour on Saturday morning? Good question. Well, I will tell you: I had to accomplish an important task — I promised to help him to devise a plan to scare Vadik-the-Bully, the biggest womanizer in our school. We needed to scare him because Kolya's former girlfriend Tanka Samokhina recently dumped my friend in favor of that disgusting asshole.

I was so concentrated on my ideas and possible ploys that I almost knocked the weird man down.

"Hold on!" he yelled, "don't run like a tractor, a meshugenner!"

And then, after glancing at my face, he asked unexpectedly, "Are you a Jew?"

His question shook me. No one had asked me this

so straight and so brazenly before. Not in the middle of the street, out of the blue.

"Yes, I am a Jew, but I prefer not to emphasize my genealogy. Why should I? I am not looking for some sort of trouble or adventure. Quite the opposite: being fair-haired and light skinned I was able to avoid many nasty slurs and jokes which, more obvious exhibitors of Semitic features, had to endure on a regular basis."

"How do you know I am a Jew?" I asked the man, slightly baffled.

"Your eyes revealed to me who you are," he said, "the expression of perpetual misery. Are you older than thirteen?"

Now, this was a real insult. Couldn't he figure out just by looking at me?

"Look," said the strange man, "we need your help. We need a tenth person."

"Who are "we" and why do you need a tenth person?"

"We — is a Jewish community. A tenth person we need for minyan. Do you know what minyan is?"

"No."

"A quorum of ten people."

And he gave me a brief, two-minute long lecture about the basics of Judaism.

"You see," he said, "we had ten people available for the morning service but one of us got sick. Today is a special occasion: a boy like you is having a bar mitzvah. It is a rare opportunity for him: he has a crazy aunt, a real meshugenner — a communist. She would never let him do that. But unfortunately for her and fortunately for the boy she is in hospital right now and his parents decided to use this occasion to accomplish the mitzvah they had been planning to do for a very long time. A few minutes ago I left the synagogue in the hope of catching an accidental Jew. I caught you. Would you help us?"

It was, by the way, Nathan Frenkel he was talking about — the boy with a crazy aunt.

Could I really refuse the plea? The burden was too high. It took priority over Kolya's quandaries.

The next couple of hours I spent listening to an unfamiliar language and examining the shabby walls of the old synagogue. At the same time I felt quite good, even like a hero, for I helped people to accomplish a great mitzvah. (I didn't know then what this word meant but nevertheless, it sounded good). And the part which came after the prayers, the kiddush, rewarded me for my efforts. Not so much the taste of the homemade delicacies or the flavor of the exceptionally fine brandy but the attitude of the congregants, the fact that everybody acted like I was one of them, on the same level. They didn't care if I was of a "drinking age" or not and that I did not have a beard, just a slight allusion to a moustache — at the festive table we were all equal.

Since then, occasionally, on the average maybe two or three times in a year, when I had no other things to do and the usual Friday night party at students' dormitory for some reason was postponed or canceled, I was coming to the synagogue. Kiddush remained my favorite part although, as the time went by, I became more and more interested in the service and prayers.

Once, after several such visits, I asked my mentor Chaim, "Could you help me to learn Hebrew? I don't understand even one word of what you are praying here. I wish I could."

And he answered, "I may teach you the prayers, young man, no problem. However, regarding the language itself I know probably not more than you do. But I know one person who might help you. His name is Mikhail, and he is a teacher of Hebrew."

This was how he introduced me to Mikhail Rothman. By that time Mikhail had already three students in his underground "ulpan": Sergey, Maya and one more man, who in a short while left USSR for Israel.

"Are you planning to go to Israel?" Mikhail asked me at our first meeting.

"No, not really," I told him, "not without my parents."

"Then what is your aim? Why do you want to study Hebrew?"

"To understand the prayers."

Mikhail glanced at me with curiosity and said, "Right. That is what you have to say to KGB operatives if they will start to interrogate you. You study Hebrew for the religious purpose. Our country declared the freedom of religion; therefore they won't be able to indict you. Do you understand? You will be fine."

He gave me a self-teaching Hebrew manual called "Mori" (which means 'my teacher') for the beginners. He probably got it from Nathan's brother, Abram. Each of us, by the way, had a different study book, and Mikhail needed to guide and direct us, to assure that we all, more or less, were on the same "page". I imagine it was not an easy task.

At the beginning I wondered where and how Mikhail himself learned his Hebrew since the Soviet government declared the language to be a fake and unlawful and banned it from all schools and universities across the Soviet Union. Where could he find a teacher? How did he get his books? Only later I found out from Sergey that Mikhail took private lessons. One woman, who studied Hebrew during Lithuanian independence in the Jewish gymnasium in Kaunas, tutored him for a while. I have no clue how well Mikhail knew the subject, but I heard rumors that when he came to Israel and started to speak Hebrew to Israeli clerks, they asked him to switch to some other language, the one they could understand.

To Mikhail's rectitude, his lessons were free; he didn't charge us even a penny. We studied Hebrew in his scruffy apartment once or twice a week, usually at the weekends. The frequency of our classes depended on everybody's scheduled and unscheduled errands, Mikhail's sporadic detentions and Laima's frequent headaches. Sometimes we had to postpone our classes for weeks, even for months.

Well, to call Mikhail's dwelling an apartment would be a bit of a stretch. He had one small room plus a kitchen and bathroom which he shared with another two families, who were complete strangers. One of his neighbors was a hunched old lady, sixty or seventy years old (nobody knew how old she was, even she herself), half-blind and half-deaf. She rarely went out of her room and even more so outside the house because she had difficulty climbing back, on the third floor, and Laima, Mikhail's wife, had to run her errands instead. The furthest room was occupied by a family of three: two adults and their five-or six-year-old son. The husband was a habitual alcoholic: almost every time we had a class, we could hear his drunken shouts, curses and swearing, hysterical screams of his wife and loud cries of the boy. Occasionally the boy would sneak into our room to hide from his mad father.

Mikhail assured us that we are all safe here: the old lady didn't hear anything, and the family of the alcoholic didn't care. We could speak Hebrew freely and openly.

I cannot say that these classes helped me a lot. First of all they dealt mostly with conversational Hebrew rather than with the prayers, and secondly, the intermittent nature of our lessons didn't help me to facilitate the acquisition of the new and difficult language.

"Don't worry," Chaim Tsypkin comforted me during one of the kiddushes. "In prayers the most important thing is not understanding but the spirit. As long as you can read... I also don't understand half of what I say but it doesn't bother me. The spirit, the feeling — that is what counts. Let me tell you: more than once these prayers have saved my life. When I was in GULAG..."

"What was most difficult for you: when you were in GULAG or in a ghetto?" I interrupted him.

"You cannot compare one to another. These are two different things. All Jews were locked in the ghetto but only few of us got into GULAG. I was one of them. You may call me a shlimazl. I was indeed a shlimazl."

"How come?"

"Well, after the war everybody needed water. Everything was destroyed and I had to repair all the broken plumbing. Not too many plumbers were available at that time and people were pulling me left and right. But look, I couldn't be simultaneously in all the places at the same time. I had to set up priorities — to whom to do first, to whom to do later. And I made a mistake. Accidently, I repaired plumbing to the wrong person. "A Yiddishe glik" — as you know. A day later, at night, KGB officers knocked at the door of my apartment: "Hey, you, accidently survived fascist, get up and face the justice!" Officially I was charged with anti-Soviet activity and sabotage. They incriminated me with the intentional delay of the restoration of the plumbing system in the city of Kaunas. The best lawyer in all Lithuania, Mr Shapiro, for whom I'd just replaced his water pipe, stepped forward to defend me. But when during my trial he rose to say something in my defense the judge interrupted him: "If I would be in your place, comrade Shapiro," she said, "I would keep my mouth shut. It is quite easy to get from your bench to the bench of the criminal you are trying, so shamelessly, to defend." To make a long story short I was sentenced to ten years of hard labor in Siberia."

"Was the labor real hard?"

Chaim filled our glasses again:

"Well, what can I say to you, my friend? Do you see how I am limping? This is the memo from that evil institution. Even during my trip to the camp I already got the taste of what was waiting for me there. We were transported in the hold compartment of the cargo ship. which normally carried coal. Inside, the compartment was constantly dark and stinky; during the whole trip I couldn't get used to the smell of the rotten food and excrement. Time and again I could hear loud heartbreaking screams of one of the prisoners.: the two hardened criminals were checking the mouths of the fellow inmates. If they could find a golden crown or a bridge, then one of them would hold the victim by the hands while another would pull the golden teeth out of the mouth with a pair of pliers. Then these criminals would exchange the crowns for a pack of cigarettes with the guards on the upper deck.

The camp, the one I was sent to, had no running water. They were bringing it from the lake some fifty kilometers away and it was never enough. For months the prisoners, even the guards, didn't have a bath, they didn't wash themselves, everybody was dirty and sick by drinking contaminated water. I noticed a small brook below the hill and figured out that there must be a spring nearby and thus the source of the freshwater. I told about my discovery to the camp commandant Major Konovalov. I said to him that if we dug a well down there, in the valley, just several meters away from the barbed wire, we should get to the water. He okayed my idea. For more than four weeks the prisoners of the camp dug the well, but the bottom of it remained as dry as a desert. Not a single drop of water. It was very frustrating. Soon everybody got angry at me. One night several hardened criminals, former murderers and bandits, approached my bunk bed and said to me, "Listen, you sneaky Jew. Why did you force us to dig this stupid well? Did you want to avoid the dirty job of cutting down the trees in the forest? Now pray; your time is over: tomorrow this well will become your grave." And I prayed to God the whole night long and fell asleep only in the morning. I was woken by the screams: "Water! Water!" I ran to the well and guess what? It was full of water. Everybody congratulated me, even the hardened criminals. The prayer saved my life, young man. That is the power of the prayer."

"It could be just a coincidence," I objected.

"Coincidence? Oh, no! It was more than just that. Listen, several months later my boss, Major Konovalov, said to me, "Get up and be ready. In two hours we will leave this nice place and travel to the Volga-Don construction site.

What was that? You, young men, have no idea what it was. But in the late Forties-early Ffties our government proclaimed it to be "the construction of the century". Basically, it was an ambitious project to connect the two great rivers Don and Volga by a canal. Stalin, personally, curated this venture; it was sort of his baby, his "swansong". Hundreds of thousands of GULAG prisoners were sent to work there. But I wasn't one of them. Instead, when we arrived at our destination, Major Konovalov led me directly to the office of the project manager General Shektilov. I was allowed to take a seat at the table just like everyone else and was treated like an equal. Everybody talked to me with respect and a polite adjutant even brought a cup of the excellent aromatic tea. I haven't drunk such a tea for centuries. And while I was drinking it the general described to me the gravity of the situation.

Apparently, the construction was coming to an end, and everything was looking pretty good. What was left to do was just to cover the bottom of a few locks with the concrete. But as soon as workers began to pump the water out of the locks, they realized the difficulty of the task: despite all their efforts the water remained at its old original level. They worked for several weeks but didn't come even close to their goal. Then a couple of professors came from Moscow, installed new, more powerful pumps with the better filters but ended with the same deplorable result: the water didn't want to leave the locks. The professors went back to Moscow to recheck their calculations. Meanwhile, last week General Shektilov received a telephone call from Stalin's main henchman, the interior minister, Lavrentiy Beria, and the latter uttered a very frightening word: "sabotage".

"In a short time many heads will start to roll if we don't achieve any progress at any time soon," concluded the general. "Major Konovalov told me about your endeavors regarding the bath business. He was extremely impressed by your abilities. He said to me: 'This guy has a real Jewish head. I want you to use your Jewish head to solve our problem. Tell me what you need — people, equipment — everything will be provided. Just get the water out of these locks!'"

So, I went to the site and made a good observation. I concluded that the reason for the problem was the Volga-river down below, on another side of the locks. It backed up the present level of water by getting in under the ground, oozing through the sand. Can you pump out the whole river? No, of course not. What to do? But then, when we (together with the workers) dug a hole about ten to twelve meters deeper than the level of the locks we found below the layer of a heavy clay another layer of sand. What if we use its absorbing capability? I ordered perforated pipes and we put them on the sides of the locks, deep into the sand and began to pump. We had to rush. The question was who would be faster: me or the Volga? Once again, I prayed to the Lord. And he heard me, and he revealed to me his compassion. For two weeks the weather stayed hot and dry. On the fourth day we pumped the water out and then the workers had enough time to pave the floor of the locks with the asphalt and concrete. The construction was completed. There was a lot of celebration. The authorities invited domestic and foreign journalists to cover the opening of "the construction of the century". They removed the barbed wire around the site, gave prisoners civilian clothes and erected a huge sign: "This is the site of the Volga-Don canal — a great achievement of the young Soviet communists". General Shektilov drank to my health. He said he was making a list of nominees for the prestigious Stalin prize and he had included my name as the inventor of the, so-called, "the new innovative method of water pumping".

"Oh! And you receive the Stalin prize? That is something, really something!"

"No, of course I didn't receive the prize, Major Konovalov did. He was genuinely upset, though. When I was explaining to him the essence of my method, the basics of which he needed to present to the award committee, he said to me: "It is not my fault, pal, you know it. But I still feel sorry for you, for the fact that you didn't receive the medal and I will do everything in my power to get you out of the prison as soon as possible." He lived up to his promise and three months later they let me to go free for the "exceptional contribution to the greatness of the Soviet Union".

Chaim poured "Maluninku" liquor once again and glanced critically at our half-empty glasses:

"We need to replenish our supplies," he said grievously. "Next time I will ask Shmulik, who is responsible for kiddushes. Why are we constantly short of "Maluninku"?"

I don't know why Chaim likes to spend so much time with me, drinking this "Maluninku". Perhaps because he is a lonely guy: his Lithuanian wife passed away several years ago and his son lives with the family far away, in the Far East, in the city of Vladivostok. Most likely because he is a lonely guy. What would be another reason?

"But your prayers didn't help you much in the Kaunas ghetto, did they?" I said continuing to interrogate him.

"Well, on one hand you might be correct," admitted Chaim, still keeping his eyes on the half-filled glasses, "but on the other hand ... look, no, that is not true. There were several occasions when they really helped me. Why go too far? The fact that I came out alive from that nightmare is the best proof, isn't it? Don't you think it was a miracle? My prayers obviously helped me; they saved me many times. Let's drink for life, my friend, the most precious thing in the world. Life is such a wonderful phenomenon. You will start to appreciate it when you get to my age, Lechaim, my friend!"

"Lechaim! But tell me how did you got out alive?" I insisted, feeling that my tongue began to move with difficulty due to the incredible amount of "Maluninku" I'd already consumed.

"Prayers. Prayers saved me. I told you."

"Why didn't they save others? Other Jews also probably prayed."

"They prayed at the wrong time. You must pray at the right time to be saved. Farshteistu? At the right time."

"What do you mean?"

"The Nazis didn't kill ghetto inmates on a daily basis, as they did in the concentration camps. There were waves. You know — mass killings and then a few quiet months until the next occasion."

"Why?"

"Because they were Germans, my friend. Germans, as you know, are prudent and meticulous people: everything must be done according to the schedule. Is killing these people on today's schedule? No? Well, then they must wait until tomorrow. Germans."

"But how were you able to survive? Personally"

"Personally? Oh, it is a long story, my friend. Let us have another drink before I tell you. Where is "Maluninku"? What a pity! We need to discharge Shmulik from his responsibilities; he doesn't fulfill..."

"But... Tell me: how did you survive?"

"Hold it. Simple. Very simple. I will tell you. Just listen. In the first days in the ghetto the commandant's deputy commander Helmut Rauca (there was such evil man — trust me) (did I tell you about him before?) collected like two hundred males, lined us up in the middle of the "Democratu" square and said with the help of the ugly Lithuanian interpreter:

"Hey, you, Jewish parasites, blood sucking layers and usurers! For too long you have been exploiting hardworking Lithuanian folks. For too long they have built you your houses, installed your plumbing, cleaned your rooms while your Jewish commissars raped their wives and daughters and brutalized their sons. Now the time has come for you crooks to pay the Arians back. Now you will be cleaning rooms and laying bricks. And don't even dare to do your job dishonestly, as you always try to do because the punishment will be severe."

Then the evil man stopped for a moment and asked: "Did any one of you ever work in the construction business?"

I and several other guys stepped forward.

"What did you do?" he asked me.

"Plumbing."

"What?"

"Plumbing."

"You are a plumber?"

"Yes."

"A Jewish plumber? Don't try to trick me, a sneaky Jew. I'll tell you what. Today you will go to my house and fix my toilet. If you won't fix it — I will hang you on this pole."

And he pointed with his finger at the lighting pole at the edge of the square.

"I don't take it easy being tricked," he added gravely, "this should be a good example for every stinky Jew, who would ever try to trick me again."

"After that day I fixed plumbing for all the German officers in the city. Yes, that was the deal. Rauca let me live for the time being. But he didn't do it for my parents and my sister. That Nazi bastard didn't let them live."

"Is that how you survived the war? Because of Rauca?"

"Because of him? Oh, give me a break. I wished him a sweet death in a pile of sugar.. He was like Amalek, a real thug. Yah. But because he was a German he was a very meticulous person. Not like our local Lithuanian bandits. These killed Jews enjoying the process. Once I heard drunken Lithuanian policemen bragging how in the town of Mariampole they "got rid of all filthy Jews". First, they killed all men and the next day, they brought their wives and their daughters to the execution site and ordered the poor women to undress and dance naked on the top of the mass grave. The earth was still moving under them; these policemen laughed when they told me. Imagine that. And then they killed the women too and buried them in the same common grave. "Join your loved ones," they wished while shooting the women in cold blood. Savages. Bastards. No, Germans didn't act this way. Rauca was not a barbarian, he belonged to a different type of murderer — an intelligent killer."

Many years later their roads almost crossed once again. Almost.

Unlike his boss Kurt Jager, who, after supervising for several months the slaughter of the innocent people, went into a prolonged nervous breakdown and later committed suicide, Helmut Rauca happened to be a much stronger person with ta much healthier nervous system. After the war he escaped to Canada and opened inn in a suburb of Toronto. He lived peacefully in his "bed and breakfast" until the late Sixties, when he was identified by one of the few remaining ghetto survivors. Germany demanded his extradition to face charges of mass murder and crimes against humanity. The Soviet Union offered to help, and the KGB invited Chaim Tsypkin to give a written testimony, which later was submitted to the Canadian government. But the Canadian authorities didn't trust the Soviet Union testimonies nor did they believe in KGB affidavits or Soviet judicial practices, and therefore refused to accept the report presented to them by Chaim Tsypkin. Because of the understandable concern they delayed the extradition of the executioner for several more years and the notorious criminal died in his own bed as an innocent man.

One of the Canadian officials explained their decision this way: "We didn't have sufficient evidence to prove that Rauca's actions indeed constituted war crimes. So, we decided that it is better for a hundred guilty people to escape than for one innocent person to be wrongfully condemned."

Unfortunately, Nazi Germany and the Soviet Union had a different approach to the notion of justice and Chaim Tsypkin, unlike Rauca, was convicted, and not only once but twice — the first time for being a Jew, when he spent three years in Kaunas ghetto, and the second time for nothing, when he spent several years more in a Siberian labor camp.

"Of course I was upset when the bastard got away," he said to me during one of our customary Kiddush conversations, "but not for myself. I am all right. But how about the others? How about the thousands of ghetto inmates: children, elderly people? How about my parents and my sister? How about them? Did you hear what kind of message Jews left on the ghetto wall on one of the buildings? This message consists of only one word: "'nekama". Nekama means: "Take revenge". Take revenge for us, they asked, atone for our sufferings. And you know what? We betrayed them. Yes, we, survived this hell and calamity, and we betrayed them."

The word "nekama" is written in blood on one of the walls in Kaunas ghetto.

"But what good would the punishment of Rauca do for his victims?" I asked Chaim. "the ancient method of justice in the form of "eye for eye" and "tooth for tooth" would not give them any satisfaction since these people don't exist any more. It wouldn't resurrect them either. Such a solution doesn't make much sense."

"Everything, every passage in the Torah makes sense, young man. You may not see it, but it is there.

God gave us the instructions because we are not smart enough to always understand the reason. Sometimes we get lost, sometimes we cannot comprehend. Let's say, for example, why he allowed the Nazis to slaughter our people? We cannot understand this. Right? That is why we need to look in the Torah."

"Is there an answer for such a question?"

"I am sure there is. We just haven't found it yet."

Our philosophical discussions about justice

This was not the last time I heard Rauca's name. Later, during one of our regular Hebrew classes, we all got embroiled in a heated debate about this man.

"Last night," Todik said, "I was listening on the radio to the Voice of Israel and they discussed the Helmut Rauca case."

(As a side note, the Soviet Union was relentlessly jamming the broadcasts of the foreign radio stations. The KGB set up powerful transmitters all over the country to produce an irritating noise making it not only illegal but totally impossible for Soviet citizens to listen to the "blatant capitalist lies and propaganda". To further ensure compliance with the Soviet laws the Soviet administration required that all radio receivers, like the extremely popular "Spidola", be tuned at the factories to a specific frequency range: from twenty-five meters and up. It erroneously assumed, that with such strict regulations, the owners of "Spidola" and other Soviet-made receivers wouldn't be able to catch the forbidden radio station programs. Thus the Soviet authorities allowed "capitalist mouthpieces" to transmit their "mendacious propaganda" outside the normal frequency range without the usual interference. Surely enough, the shrewd capitalists immediately took advantage of this KGB blunder and Todik's friends at the radio repair shop got extremely busy in rewiring "Spidola" electrical schemes to accept radio waves below twenty-five meters range. No doubt, their job was illegal and pretty risky, but they were getting more than ten times their regular salaries and the business was booming: the wait time to retrofit a receiver with the illegal wiring exceeded many months. Todik, meanwhile, was extremely proud to be able to get the latest news ahead of everybody else).

"Who was that man, Rauca?' asked Maya and Sergey, both unfamiliar with the issue.

Todik gave us a brief outline, and then Mikhail explained that there were many cases like this.

"This Nazi, Rauca followed the orders of his superiors," he said, "and the Canadian system of justice couldn't handle such a kind of challenge. It was unprepared. In fact, the justice system in many countries, particularly in the West, has failed miserably when it dealt with the Nazi war crimes."

"In which way?" asked Maya.

"In many. I myself know a number of such cases."

"Tell us," said Sergey.

"Well, one case involved the former commandant of the Nazi death camps Sobibor and Treblinka. Franz Stangl responsible for the murders of almost a million people. After the war he escaped to Syria using a Red

Cross passport and then from there to Brazil, where he was joined by his family. He didn't try to conceal his true identity and was registered in the Austrian consulate in Sao Paulo under his real name. It took ten years for the Austrian government to issue the official warrant for his arrest. Nevertheless, the Austrian foreign ministry (headed at that time by the Jewish socialist Bruno Kreisky, who later became Austrian chancellor) didn't move a finger to comply with the request of its government and didn't ask Brazilian authorities for his extradition. Only six years later, after Stangl was traced down by Simon Wiesenthal, who made his existence public, was he finally extradited from Brazil to Germany where he was tried in court, found to be guilty in murdering nine hundred thousand people and sentenced to life imprisonment. One year later he died there from heart failure. During the trial, the defense lawyer made the same argument as in the case of Rauca, mainly that he just followed the orders of his superiors. Stangl expressed the same opinion.. "My conscience is clear," he said, "I was simply doing my duty."

"Wasn't this the same line of defense during the Nuremberg trials?" asked Sergey.

"You are correct. During those trials all the Nazis claimed that they were not guilty because they just had to follow the orders of their superiors. What is the problem? The problem is that this chain of command could lead up and up and then there would be only one criminal in the whole world —Hitler himself. To avoid such absurdity the prosecutors declared that following unlawful orders is also a crime."

"Is it not?"

"Of course, not. Take, for example, the fact, that at the time the Nazis followed those orders this ruling didn't even exist. So, how could they break it if it wasn't there? Nonsense, absurd. Besides there is an obvious problem with the logic as well. These Nazi criminals, in fact, acted quite lawfully, if you take into consideration the laws of Nazi Germany. But which laws are they supposed to follow — Great Britain? The Soviet Union? They lived in Germany."

"But they still were criminals, weren't they?"

"Of course they were."

"A lot of confusion here," concluded Todik, "This issue is highly convoluted. Why don't we drop it?"

"Indeed," agreed Laima, "it is boring. I will make a coffee for everyone."

She yawned and left us, presumably for the kitchen.

"Laima is right," remarked Todik thoughtfully, "let's talk about something else."

"I think the correct judgment must be based on the moral factors," suggested Maya timidly, "I mean in order to resolve this dilemma. Yes, each person must have the moral responsibilities as well as legal ones. Don't' they?"

"Oh, give me a break!" I couldn't remain quiet

any longer, after such pronounced nonsense "Which ones? The ones you take from the "Moral code of the Builder of Communism"?

"Indeed," Sergey agreed. "Everyone has his own, set of moral values distinct from the others. Religion or ideology determines those benchmarks for each particular individual; it defines what is right or what is wrong. And since there are many different and often mutually exclusive religions and ideologies, I agree, it is impossible to determine who is correct and why someone is correct based only on a moral point of view."

"Maybe we should look at this from Kant's position on a free will and pure reason," I suggested.

Nobody, though, responded to my remark since nobody, including me, had any idea what Kant meant in defining those objects.

"There's a lot of confusion here," repeated Todik.

"There is no confusion," assured Mikhail. "Look, the issue could be resolved quite simply. All you need to do is to free yourself from the trivial way of thinking. Answer me this question: could someone be guilty of anything if he or she has no control over it? Could a messenger, for example, be responsible for a message he delivers?"

"No, I guess not," Sergey answered instead of Todik, "but what it has to do with the Nazi crimes?"

"Hold it! So, do you agree with me that each person is responsible for the action he commits only when he has a free choice?"

"Well, yes... sure"

"And is he not responsible when he doesn't have a free choice?"

"Nazi officers didn't have a free choice," asserted Sergey.

"In other words, you, Serezha, are saying that Nazi officers cannot be held responsible?"

"Theoretically... no"

"But they were?"

"Well, somebody must be — the crime was committed."

"Indeed. Then let me ask you this question: if we concluded that in order to commit a crime the presence of the free choice is absolutely necessary then it means that Nazis had to have it. Right?"

"Yes, it is true, they had to have it... but we already determined that they didn't."

"When?"

"What — when? When they committed a crime"

"And when did they commit a crime? Wasn't it at the same time they received the order?"

"Yes."

"So, at the time they committed the crime they didn't have a free choice?"

"That is right."

"But to commit a crime they had to have it?"

"True"

"And the crime was indeed committed?"

"Yes, for sure it was."

"Then what is the conclusion we should make from this?'

"What?"

"To commit a crime they had to have a free choice. Right? But at the time they committed those crimes they didn't have it. Right? On the other hand the crime was committed. Did I miss anything? No? Then, what conclusion can we make? Doesn't it mean that they had to have a free choice at some other time, not when they received the order?"

"Well, I guess this could be a logical assumption. But when was it? The time, I mean?"

"Now I have another question for you: did all Nazis commit war crimes?"

"No, of course not all of them."

"Which ones of them didn't? Okay, I will help you. The vast majority of the war crimes were committed by a certain group of Nazis. Only by a certain group. All the heads of the concentration camps, all the commanding officers of the Einsatzgruppen and so on. They all were members of the SS (The organization was called "Schutzstaffel")."

"So?"

"So... People joined that organization freely. Correct? Nobody forced them to do it. In joining this organization did they obey someone's orders?"

"I see what you mean. But how could you blame all members of the SS if only some of them participated in murders?" asked Maya.

"First of all, we should not blame them all. The members of the SS exercised their free choice not only once. The first time they did it when they joined that sinister organization. Right? Then they did it again while being promoted to higher and higher ranks. Nobody forced them to do it — correct? Nevertheless, at some point they willingly accepted the position which required them to carry out the orders of their superiors and thus commit mass murders."

"But Misha, Mikhail, look, not all SS officers of the same rank committed murders. Am I wrong?"

"No, you are correct. But this is irrelevant. As I said before, they committed a crime not by killing somebody but by accepting a certain position in the SS organization. Do you understand? The fact that one of them was killing people and another one was just counting how many the first one killed doesn't make any difference. It was a gamble, like a lottery. Their superior could exchange their roles in no time at all. Then the second one would be guilty instead of the first. But the justice shouldn't depend on chances. Or should it?"

"What you are saying," interjected Sergey, "is that Nazi crimes should be judged by the rank of the officers in the SS organization and not by what actually they did or didn't during the war?"

"Precisely. What they did is irrelevant since they all carried out the orders. However the nature of those orders depended on their place in the Nazi hierarchy as well as within German society in general and it was not accidental. It came as the result of a free choice those people made before they accepted the orders."

"Your suggestions, Mikhail, are too unconventional," admitted Todik. "Why does it take so long for Laima to make just a few cups of coffee?"

"I agree," said Maya, "they are unconventional. It means that the court must convict people for their place in society rather than for their actions. It also looks like a collective punishment. At least to me it looks that way."

"First of all, they all would be convicted for their actions — for joining the SS, because it was an action. And secondly — there is no other way to achieve justice if you want a free choice to be a necessary factor in determining someone's culpability."

"It still looks strange," said Maya, "I mean to sentence someone for joining the SS just because another member of the SS of the same rank committed a crime. It's as if a director of one company steals the money you must convict directors of all companies. Doesn't sound correct to me!"

"You are talking about apples and oranges," Mikhail confronted her, "For the dictatorial regimes, like Nazi Germany or the Soviet Union, where relations between people are or were based on the military rather than civilian code, where all citizens are divided between masters and their servants, on superiors and their subordinates, the usual principles of a judgment don't work."

"Why?"

"Because... If we just look at the actions of individuals, we will come to absurd conclusions. Take, for example, a Nazi officer who at the train station by the name of Auschwitz was carrying a selection: sending some of the arrived prisoners to the right and the rest to the left. If we take into account only his action, then we must declare this officer to be the righteous among righteous for he saved more Jews than any Schindler ever did. However we hold him to be a criminal, not much different from those who led the prisoners to the gas chambers. This is a problem of a generalization, of our inability to apply different criteria for a different set of values, a belief that civilization is everywhere the same and its laws are also the same and universal. Using this preposterous assumption we would come to the absurd conclusion that, in order to achieve logical decisions, we need to deny the logic itself as happened during the Nuremberg trials. We cannot replace true justice with our convenience. There is nothing universal in this world, every case is unique and specific, every nation, every situation and even every human being is distinct from any other and therefore all the declarations which have in them the term "universal" must be discarded and abolished."

"But don't we need something in common, some

kind of guidance that we all should comply with?" asked Maya.

"No. The guidance is unique to every specific group of people. Not universal. For communists — it is Marxism-Leninism, for us — it is the Torah."

No doubt, Mikhail's conclusions as Todik correctly noticed, were not too conventional.

But on the other hand, perhaps, if the Canadian court accepted his arguments then maybe Rauca would not be able to trick our trust in justice with such impunity? Maybe, in that case, we would not betray the memory of his victims? And maybe Chaim Tsypkin would finally come to peace with himself also? Who knows? Mikhail's opinion remained just his opinion and nothing else.

Thus, the question about accountability, justice and punishment stays open.

Maya Katz (again)

In our everyday life we usually don't think about things like that. We have more immediate and urgent issues to take care of, like unsettled family matters, our relations with co-workers, health problems, the unfinished guest room in the basement... many different things. In other words, we have no time for the philosophical and moralistic whims, for questions regarding betrayal and retribution. Usually we don't have them. But not always.

Several years ago I bumped into Maya Katz d in Orlando Disney World where I went together with my family to spend our daughter's unscheduled school vacation.

At first, I didn't even recognize her. She had changed so much over the years. In defiance of the laws of nature she became more attractive, more charming, and more confident than she had ever been. Time had been good to her and it was as if the old tale about the ugly duckling had suddenly come true.

When we met she wore an elegant hat with a wide brim, Gucci sunglasses and a trendy gown coming down to her ankles while her sparkly diamond earrings enhanced her usual smile. She looked like a queen that had just stepped down from her throne.

Maya recognized me first.

"Wow-whoa," she screamed across the street, "Leo!" calling me by the made-up name known only to my very old friends, the forgotten relic of those long-gone days. At first I didn't even realize that her shout was directed at me.

'Hi, Leo, is that you?" she repeated once again, a little bit confused by the bewildered smile on my face.

"Maya? Is that you? How could it be?" I was so surprised I could find the words to express my amusement.

"Leo!"

"Maya! I still don't believe it is you!"

"And I don't believe it is you!"

We hugged and kissed each other.

I have to admit: we are living in a really small world.

She introduced me to her son Ilan and I to my family.

Then we spent the entire day together. My wife unselfishly let me go, to enjoy the company of my old friend while Maya's son Ilan joined my family for a whole day. Everybody had a good time.

I told Maya about my present life, about my family and my daughter, while she shared with me her experience.

She said that her last name was not Katz any more

but von Shinkenfeld and that she lives with her husband, who is almost forty years older than her, in Switzerland, in the German part of the country. They met at an art show in Jerusalem where he came to acquire some artwork at the bargain price.

"Which artwork? Your paintings?" I asked Maya.

"Mine? Sort of. But not in the sense you may think," she said and smiled meekly.

And then she told me her story.

When she arrived in Israel she and Sergey almost immediately separated since their fictional marriage was never intended to last more than a day or two beyond the USSR border. Sergey was not attracted to Maya and she was not impressed by him.

At first she didn't even realize that she was pregnant. For a couple of months she stayed with her parents in the center of absorption and then she came to the conclusion that she couldn't stay with them any longer. The reason was mainly her crazy dad. Maya said she lost all patience and couldn't stand him any more. Even back in Lithuania he had a complicated character but in Israel he became totally intolerable. All kinds of bureaucratic procrastinations and delays, difficulty with the new language and odd customs, excruciating heat of the brutal Israeli summer and insensitive (in his eyes) behavior of his older brother — all these issues drove him into madness. On top of his uncontrolled outbursts, Maya's mother also constantly scolded her for ending relations with

Sergey.

"Look at yourself," she was saying, "Look at the mirror — do you realize how old you are? You are almost thirty. Who will take you? Ah? Tell me. Who? Who will be that noble person? You are not rich enough to have the luxury to marry late."

Maya ran away from them.

She settled in a small apartment in the impoverished South Tel-Aviv neighborhood near the central bus station and began to work as a janitor and home cleaner. She dropped her classes in ulpan, a Hebrew language school for the new immigrants, and gave up on the idea of getting a nurse license. Rather, she still nurtured her childhood dream of becoming an artist, a painter, to fulfil her lifelong urge and desire. Her uncle, dad's older brother, loaned her some money, so she could travel to Jerusalem to apply for the famous art academy Bezalel.

During her interview with an adviser, a well-known Israeli sculptor, the elderly man suddenly interrupted her revelations with an odd question.

"I want to ask you one delicate question, young lady," he said, "Forgive me if it may sound a little bit too brazen, but are you pregnant?"

Maya was utterly surprised. Not even two weeks had passed since she found out about the pregnancy herself.

"How do you know it?" she asked in amusement.

"I am an artist," he said, "my job is to notice in

humans the details they themselves sometimes hardly might notice. So, are you pregnant?

And after she confirmed his guess, he said, "The reason I asked you is because you are working now as a janitor. Hard job, little money. We have a special arrangement here, in our college, for people like you. Certain financial assistance if I can put it bluntly. Plus the government will compensate the biggest portion of your tuition since you are a new immigrant (ole hadash). However I want to propose to you something else."

He waited for a second to see what effect his words had on her and then continued, "We need a model for our drawing classes. Do you understand what I mean? We need a young lady. The one who previously worked here had to leave us after giving birth. Our drawing classes need, specifically, a pregnant woman. Would you be willing to take her place?"

He paused to let Maya absorb his words.

She definitely needed time to consider such a weird proposal. No longer than a week ago, after she found that she was pregnant, she made a final and indubitable decision to perform an abortion. And now this...

"Is it necessary to be pregnant?" she asked meekly.

"It is indispensable... That is what we need."

And seeing her hesitancy the adviser scurried to

explain all the benefits she would receive by agreeing to the offer:

"All your art classes will be for free. Not just for you but for your child as well, if he or she decides to dedicate himself to the art. Very good, excellent salary, nice conditions. Much better than you have at this moment. You won't be sorry, young lady."

But she still was hesitating. Should she tell him that she was not married? That she had concerns about her baby's future and therefore wanted to end her pregnancy? That she is new to this country and doesn't yet know all the ins and outs. That she was really, really scared. Would he care about all these issues?

"You don't need to answer me right now," he assured her, "go home, relax, think about it... When you decide give us a call. Here is my telephone number."

The advisor would not be an advisor if he would not be able to give the advice.

She went back home, to her closet, which her landlady called "an apartment", looked in the mirror, as her mother urged her to do, checked the schedule for the cleaning appointments, remembered the snooty faces of her employers, the few tattered shekels in her hands and picked up the phone.

"Was it a difficult job?" I asked Maya.

"At the beginning. I didn't know how I could hide from the shame, from the embarrassment that I felt standing naked in front of the students, when they, complete strangers to me, studied and scrutinized all the intimate parts of my body. Nobody touched me but still... it was very unpleasant if I can put it mildly. Imagine someone examines your body with the magnifying glass. How would you feel? But after a while I got used to being exposed like that. I stopped paying attention to the students and to my naked body. Instead I was thinking about my unborn child, about my baby, and how he would look and how he would talk, what we are going to do together and how much assistance I would be able to provide him in his future life. I also was thinking about the pictures I was going to paint, about my expositions and public recognition. It was about my coming fame. These were sweet dreams, but the time was passing fast."

"Did you achieve some of them?"

"Oh, yah, Ilan exceeded all my expectations."

"I mean — your paintings."

Maya laughed:

"Oh, no, these are still in my dreams. One day... one day. Maybe."

"Why? You painted so great. I still have my portrait..."

"There were several reasons. First I realized...how to say it? I looked at the works of the other students and I compared them to mine. It was not too easy to come to the inconvenient conclusion, trust me. It didn't happen in an instant. It took me a long, a very long time. But I tried to be objective, you know... I always do. Besides this, true art requires a lot of time. And I didn't have it. First came Ilan, then Boris…"

"Who?'

"Boris. My husband. Boris von Sheinkenfeld."

"Is he Russian? "

"Oh, no, he is a Swiss. Just his first name is Russian. He is an art collector. He came to Israel to look for a bargain at the time I was still working in Bezalel Academy. Someone told him that due to the flood of Russian emigres to Israel he could find a "chef-oeuvre" at the price of a junk. He visited the art exhibition of the Bezalel Academy graduates and saw my portraits."

"And?"

"I was naked. Pregnant. And he fell in love with me."

"You are kidding."

"No. These were his words. Somehow, I don't know how, he found out that I am alone, not married, and he asked the exhibition manager to help him to meet me. Something impressed Boris in my portraits."

"What?"

"I don't know. He said my eyes. Or my posture. I don't know. He said that he as an art collector and art guru can distinguish unusual traits in every human being. He said I was the most unusual person he'd ever met."

Strange. I never noticed anything unusual in Maya.

"We spent several weeks together, went to restaurants, movies, had some fun. And then he asked me to marry him".

"And you agreed? Just like that?"

"What should I do? He was forty years older — that is true. But I was almost thirty myself and in the eighth month of pregnancy. My future as an artist was dubious. No money, no future. He agreed to adopt my child; he was rich, he had a huge estate in the Swiss Alps. What would you do in my place? Since I came to Israel I became a practical person, not the same as I was in Lithuania. Yes, I agreed."

"Is he still okay now?"

"Oh, yah. He is still all right. Nobody can even guess his age — because he looks so young. We sleep in separate rooms, though, on separate beds. When he has an urge he comes to my room, when I have an urge I come to him. Do you know what I mean? Lately it has happened extremely rarely. But is this a major thing? No. I could be unfaithful to him — that is true, no question: I had several opportunities. There was once an artist, for example... young, passionate. But look, why? Why should I cheat on him? Boris is a good person; he loves Ilan and treats him like his own child. And I am not a romantic teenager too any more: I have an obligation not to risk my son's future."

Her eyes became contemplative.

"You don't have common children with Boris, do you?"

"We did. But he was born prematurely."

She sighed.

"Boris has several children of his own," she added, "from his previous marriages and they occasionally visit us. We both got used to each other and live now quite comfortable lives. I have nothing to complain about."

She sighed once again.

"I am not the same girl I was," she said after a short pause.

I'd noticed it already, I wanted to say to her.

We sat quietly for several minutes.

"Did Ilan ever see his father?" I asked her.

"Only on his deathbed. At first I wanted to find Sergey to let him pay for his child. But then Boris and I decided not to do that. Boris said we didn't need his money."

"But maybe Sergey didn't know he had a child?"

"He did."

She sighed one more time.

"Ilan cannot forgive him. Not yet. Poor Ilan."

We sat mutely for a while.

"Do you know that he was killed?" she asked me suddenly.

"Yes, I heard it."

And again, we didn't say a word for several minutes.

"Do you know anything about the others?" I asked her finally, "I lost all the contacts."

"I saw Mikhail during Sergey's funeral. He is the same as he was back in Lithuania. Idealist. Years didn't change him at all. Strangely enough, I still had some feelings toward him. There was a time I was an idealist too in Russia. What a nice time it was."

"Indeed. I, myself, often recall those days. I think they were the best days of my life. We were young... Do you remember you went to Moscow?"

"When?"

"To see the Mona Lisa exposition."

"Oh, yah, of course I remember. But I was late then: by the time I arrived the exposition had already moved back to France. Now I am coming every year to Paris to catch up with what I missed. Not a big deal any more. Still, I am longing for those old days. Don't you? How much fun did we have then! It is not nostalgia per se but ... Do you remember our classes in Mikhail's apartment? How Pimple played the guitar, and we all sang Hebrew and Russian songs? How have we argued all the time? And how Mikhail's drunk neighbors constantly screamed in the other room?"

"I wonder what happened to their poor boy."

"When I visited Lithuania someone told me he became a homeless drug addict."

"You visited Lithuania? When? How many times have you been there?"

"Several. It is not too far from Switzerland."

"And...?"

"What can I tell you? Sure, it is not the same. I

went to the "Coffee and Ice cream" restaurant. Remember it? The restaurant is still there but the public is not the same. Nobody argues about books and movies. Diners sit quietly with smartphones in their hands. And "Laisves Alleya" is not the same either. Do you remember those warm summer evenings when the crowds of people slowly strolled, met their friends and chatted? Not any more. No. The street is almost empty, just a few random folk passing here or there. It feels so blank and depressing. Do you remember those elderly Jews who were tattling on the benches, gossiping and arguing about everything in the world? They did it so loud that you could hear their voices several blocks away. No Jews in Kaunas any more and no Yiddish. It is all in the past."

"Anything else? Any more changes? Perhaps more positive?"

"Well, they removed the Lenin statue and instead put Vytautas the Great on the square across from central park. There is also a memorial to Romas Kalanta in front of the Musical Theatre at the site where he set himself on fire. Do you remember the spring when he did it?"

"Oh, yah, sure I remember it. They were showing on TV riots in Northern Ireland at that time: burning Belfast, crowds of shouting demonstrators. But you come out on the street and you would see exactly the same things: burning tires, broken windows, protesters with the national Lithuanian flags screaming "freedom to Lithuania", wounded people on the walkways... Unfortunately, the world knew nothing about these events, unlike Northern Ireland."

"The world sees only the things the media shows them. It is ignorant to everything outside it. And Soviet authorities tried very hard to conceal the protests."

"And to prevent similar disturbances in the future. Each year on the day of the anniversary, there were more disguised KGB agents on the streets than there were normal folk. Apparently the protesters scared a lot of our political bosses. I am glad they finally achieved their goal and Lithuania again became an independent country. Good for them. Have you been in the other parts of Lithuania, besides Kaunas?"

"Yes. I visited Druskininkai, Palanga, Vilnius. Same thing. Not as it was. Sad. We went to Ponary forest, to the execution site, where thousands of Vilnius Jews were murdered during World War Two..."

"Do you remember how we went there many years ago? We were able to gather several hundred men and women from Kaunas and Vilnius to attend the memorial service on the anniversary of the mass execution. Do you remember that event?"

"Yes, I do. I do remember how the officials removed all public buses to prevent us from coming there. Some of us took taxis to get there but we walked on foot almost ten miles."

"They later claimed that all their buses suddenly

and simultaneously broke off."

"Broke off? Ha-ha. On the other hand, who knows, maybe they indeed broke off? Do you remember how overcrowded they were during workdays?"

"Oh, yah, I certainly remember these proletarian means of transportation. Sure. How not to remember them? They were packed to a point when nobody could get on at the bus stops. And then the bus driver would accelerate his vehicle for a couple of seconds and then abruptly halt it. The inertia would draw the passengers toward the front of the bus freeing some space in the back and giving a chance for a few more lucky guys to get in. Everybody got squeezed like fish in a barrel."

"It was a heaven for pickpockets and old perverts. They groped young girls if you didn't know it."

"I have no doubt they had the opportunity. Do you remember the joke? Sir, could you, please, move your umbrella? You are poking into my butt. Sorry, young lady, but it is not an umbrella."

"Ha-ha-ha. No, this is the first time I've heard it. But on the hand, it was warm during the winter. Do you remember? Sometimes we rode those buses just to warm up. They had some advantages too."

"Except that they were exceedingly warm in the summer. Extremely hot, as a matter of fact. Everybody sweated and smelled like rotten fish. And there was no place even to step aside, no escape from that reek."

"Once I remember one guy got on. He probably ate a pound of garlic before boarding. Imagine, there was a meter of a circle around him completely free of people."

"Ha-ha. He had to be a smart guy. Probably a Jew. Do you remember how local Lithuanians called those who smelled garlicky? You smell like a Jew. Do you remember that?"

"Yes, of course, I remember that expression. And many others. Not overly flattery. Don't remind me of them — it was so long ago. I want to forget those nasty expressions. Better to think about something nicer. How we celebrated Jewish holidays in Kaunas synagogue, for example. Or how we read the *Exodus* book in the park behind the restaurant. Do you remember it?"

"Listen, Maya... I wanted to ask you... I'd wanted to ask you for a long time. Do you know what happened after that, after that night?"

"No, what?"

"I didn't tell you before. I was summoned to the KGB office on "Laisves Alleya." Some captain... I forgot his name... Belousov? I think — Belousov. Well, he came from Moscow to interrogate me, to find out who gave us the *Exodus* book. Have you heard anything about that?"

"Something."

"What something? From whom?"

"Why do you worry so much? Many years have

passed."

"Someone betrayed us. Someone told the KGB we read the book: a KGB informer. I want to find out who that person was."

"Why? What difference does it make? Will it change anything?"

"Do you know who he was?"

"Don't you know yourself?"

"Me? No. I can make only a guess...Was it... Sergey?"

"What is the difference? Why Sergey?"

"Well, he didn't know he was Jewish until he was sixteen."

"So what? Many people didn't know they were Jewish until they were older. I found out that I am Jewish only when I was six or seven."

"Who did you think you were?"

"I don't know, I didn't think about it. My parents spoke Yiddish at home, but I didn't pay attention. Well, not that I didn't pay ... I just didn't think about it. I didn't relate it... how to say this? They could speak any language. My dad was a communist and he didn't want us to celebrate Jewish holidays at home but my grandmother (when she was still alive) every year was bringing poppy seed cookies on Purim and matzo bread during Passover. Someone privately baked it in Kaunas synagogue. Or in his or her home... I didn't know and I didn't care. I thought everybody ate matzo bread on Passover. In other words, I had no idea that we were Jews or somehow different from our neighbors until I was six or, maybe even, seven."

"What happened then?"

"Then... One day I was playing in our backyard with the kids of my age who came from the project house across the street. They ran around the yard and sang a new song: "kike, kike, ugly stinky kike". I instantly joined them and began to run and sing that song with them. I thought it was a funny song. And then suddenly (it took me a little time) I realized that the words were directed toward me. Why? I thought. What did I do to these kids? Why am I a stinky kike? I am not stinky... I began to cry — it looked very unfair to me: I didn't consider myself to be a bad person. There was an old lady sitting on the bench in the yard. She looked at me with pity and said to the children, "Hai, you, nasty gangsters, leave this little kike alone." And the kids changed the words of the song: "kike, kike, little stinky kike". I had no doubt any more. They were singing about me, I ran home to my grandmother crying: "Grandma, grandma, I don't want to be a stinky kike." And she said: "Don't cry my little meidele; now you know who you are." That is how I found out that I am Jewish. You may ask other Jews from Russia. Almost everybody will tell you a similar story."

"True, I had a similar incident when I was in the third grade."

"See, Sergey was not unique."

"Right, perhaps... but still not at the age of sixteen... on the other hand... could it be Pimple?"

"Pimple? Why Pimple? He gave us the book if you remember. Why would he inform on himself? It would be silly, wouldn't it? By the way, he became quite a famous person in Israel. There were articles in the newspapers about him. Have you read them?"

"Articles? No. In which way did he become famous?"

"Not in the way you may wish. Remember, even back in Lithuania he showed some remarkable business skills. He had a talent to deal with people and a lot of charisma. Sometimes I wished I could have his character. Unfortunately, he didn't use it the right way. In Israel he befriended several high ranking officials from the Israeli Labor party and got a position as a financial accountant in the "Sokhnut" organization. He stole from that organization hundreds of thousands of shekels and then he was caught, tried, convicted of embezzlement, and spent several years in Israeli prison. Upon release he moved to Moldova, with one of his new friends (I think he met him there, in prison) and got involved in porno business: he became some kind of an expert in uncovering beautiful young women willing for pennies to perform in dirty porno movies. This business brought him a lot of money, but it didn't last for too long. One day a competing gang of scoundrels tried to assassinate him, but he miraculously survived. Then he escaped to

Belgium..."

"Why to Belgium and not to Israel?"

"He didn't like Israel. When I met him at Sergey's funeral he told me that although the country by itself is modern and nice, it has one major flaw: too many Jews live in it. Therefore he went to Belgium, a country with fewer Jews. He settled in the city of Antwerp and changed his profession to become a diamond exchange broker. He worked for some time for a shady corporation without a name. And then he decided to open his own business. He went to Africa, to a country which didn't have any Jews at all, called Sierra-Leone, to buy cheap diamonds. And he got into some trouble: either he gave a bribe to the wrong person or didn't share his profit or whatever and was arrested once again. I believe he is still in a Sierra-Leone prison."

"Back in Lithuania I had a suspicion that he might end this way. Poor guy."

"I think he still has his millions"

"What is the point to have these millions in prison?"

"Well, still better than nothing. So, you don't think he was an informer?"

"What difference does it make?"

"Because if it was not him then who else could it be?"

"You know what, Leo? Let's leave it. Ah? Let's forget it. Will you? It won't change anything right now. What is the point of looking backwards? All people make mistakes."

"But not all of them repent them."

"It is always easier to judge someone else. We shouldn't dwell on our past. We live in new countries; we live new lives. We all had changed, and the things had changed too. Let's remember only the good parts of our former lives."

I don't know what Maya had in mind while saying these words.

There was one issue which we didn't touch on during our discussion at all, as if it was some kind of taboo, a germ or a deadly disease: it was the issue of our own culpability. We didn't utter even one word about our meeting in Sergey parents' apartment many years ago. And we didn't mention his parents at all. Not even one word. It was as if we came to a silent agreement between ourselves that Sergey made his decision exclusively on his own and we didn't play any part in it.

I was waiting when Maya will ask me what my answer to Lieutenant Belousov enquiry was.

But she didn't ask it. Instead she said: "Now tell me about yourself. How was your trip to a free world and how you settled in a new country?"

My voyage to a free world

And here is what I recounted to her.

Unlike all my close friends I didn't immigrate to Israel. After leaving the USSR my parents changed their minds and decided to move to the USA, to the country of the greater opportunities and wealthier relatives.

On our way to the new world we made several memorable stops: first, for a couple weeks in the Austrian capital Vienna and then the second, much longer one, in the Italian city of Ladispoli.

The trip itself had two opposing elements. On the one hand it is never easy to move from one place to another. The relocation becomes even more challenging when you must leave the country of your birth and move to a land of strange customs and unfamiliar language. It is even more difficult if this new place has a completely different political system. And it becomes unbearably hard when you know in advance that there is no way back, that this is it and you have no chance to see the place you have lived for so long, that you will never be able to visit the graves of your deceased ancestors; and that from now on you are nobody, a stateless person, a person without a country and without a home, and that the folks who are waving to you "goodbye" from the crowded railroad platform — they are waving to you for the last time in your life and you will never see them again: not your relatives, not your friends, not your beloved ones ...

It had to be a tough experience.

But all these difficulties cannot even be compared to the situation when on top of all the above mentioned hurdles you are in complete darkness regarding the nature of your destination.

Columbus, I think, had a better knowledge of America than we did. Soviet propaganda accomplished a great job in nurturing our ignorance. All we knew about the American continent was that it consisted of the "stone jungles": treeless filthy towns, lit by billboards and glitzy advertisements and inhabited by drug addicts and criminal bullies; that those Americans who hadn't yet committed suicide were preparing to do so in the near future, and that even such an outgoing and friendly personality like Santa, instead of nice Christmas gifts, was delivering to the desperate residents more and more bad news about upcoming calamities and misery.

But on the other hand, we had entered the world, which was forbidden to us, utterly unknown, the world of the endless adventures and unexpected discoveries, the whole universe without duplicitous informers and eavesdropping devices, free from hypocrisy of political correctness and unquestionable obedience. I bet

American astronauts were not as thrilled when they stepped for the first time on the surface of the moon as we did when we disembarked from a dusty train carriage on the concrete floor of the Vienna train station. Everything there was new and exhilarating.

Later in our life we traveled to many places trying to amuse ourselves with the views of Grand Canyon and Niagara Falls, with the natural beauty of the Hawaiian Islands and Swiss Alps, to enjoy architectural marvels of London, Paris and Rome; we also went on African safari and visited the North Pole, jumped on parachutes and kayaked swift waters but never, even remotely, experienced the same level of emotions that we felt looking at the noisy, busy streets of the Austrian capital for the first time. Are these the same streets that Austrian Jews were cleaning on their knees many years ago? In this place we realized for the first time what the word "freedom" means.

After the initial shock endured in Austria we moved to a sun-sunken Italy and spent several months in that beautiful country waiting for the visas from the American embassy. Although the exciting time continued, the Jewish organization HIAS, which took temporary care of stateless immigrants, has provided us with only essential necessities, such as basic food and lodging. Anything beyond these items we had to obtain ourselves. And there were so many temptations.

Our financial situation, however, was not particularly great: everything we had earned during our entire lives: our savings, jewelry, private collections and so on we had to leave behind, in our former country. The Soviet government didn't allow you to take beyond its border any object which could exceed a certain, actually quite low, value, since it considered every item in the Soviet Union to be the property of the nation and not of the individuals. So, besides forty pounds of luggage (where each piece could not surpass some, precisely defined, value), a hundred dollars per person and a good education most of the immigrants had no other means to start their new lives.

Back in the days which we, immigrants, christened "Roman holidays" we had no clue what was waiting for us ahead, how we were going to survive in our new and unfamiliar home and therefore we had to be extremely prudent and careful with our money. Every penny was counted and recounted. We understood: a hundred dollars wouldn't last for too long.

No wonder, instead of necessities, the business-savvy immigrants packed their luggage with all kinds of commercial stuff, anything they could find in the impoverished and chronically plagued by shortages, government stores, spending long hours in lines, under snow and biting wind, at subzero temperatures, to buy simple things like fine china or a set of colorfully painted wooden spoons or some kinds of mechanical gadgets. Now the time came to reap the rewards.

Every Sunday morning a motley crowd of

refugees was heading toward the main Rome flea market at Porta Portese in the hope to cash in on their merchandise. Former doctors, teachers and rocket scientists were lining up along Via Portuense offering to the lofty Italian customers linen dish towels, matryoshkas, ballet slippers, cans with red caviar, "Stolichnaya" vodka and many other things. The assortment of the goods was as diverse as immigrants themselves: from the Red Army underwear and to the diamond cutting tools.

The neighbors in our apartment on Via del Mare, for example, (we shared one apartment, just lived in two separate rooms) were folk from the provincial city of Tomsk. The head of the family in his previous vocation worked as a leading baritone in the local opera theatre. He brought to Italy two suitcases of condoms. I still remember his thick and strong voice gracefully reverberating over the flea market:

"Comprare, comprare Sovetico anti-bambino fenominale!"

I wonder what Soviet customs officers were thinking when they checked his luggage during his departure or if he found any brave customer for his risky product.

Prior to our arrival the cleaning of the windshields of passing cars was also quite popular business. For example, when a car stopped at the regulated intersection a feverish immigrant, with a brush in one hand and purse for the money in another, jumped forward and started to wipe off all the real and imaginary dirt.

By the time we arrived, however, this activity went into decline, first, due to the huge number of competitors and secondly, because by that moment local Italian drivers had already learned a few Russian words and using their limited but extremely expressive vocabulary sent annoying cleaners back to the country of their origin and didn't pay them even a penny.

Not all refugees, of course, acted this way. Soviet communists did a great job of creating a new human being (they called him "a builder of communism"), a person, who was supposed to give to the society as much as he could and take from it as much as he needed.

For that purpose the Soviet Union employed two, not related to each other, institutions. One was the government, and another was the "people". These two entities operated separately and in theory their relations should be mimicking the relation between a dog and his owner. The owner takes care of the dog, feeds him, gives him shelter, pets him (if the dog behaves well) and so on. In exchange the dog must be loyal to his owner, obey his orders, and defend him from his enemies.

In reality, however, it didn't work that well. Both, the government, and the people, relentlessly cheated each other, and deceived, as much as they could, in order to get more for less. This mentality eventually spread over the entire population, particularly among its most intelligent and vibrant part. The coolest became the ones who could trick everybody else. Honesty and integrity turned into a target of many nasty jokes and the most prized trait became the ability to dupe and swindle other human beings. KGB informers and snitches, although despised and hated by most of the population, nevertheless, blossomed due to the hefty benefits they were receiving from the government agencies. Besides all of these, the laws of the country were made in such a way that the law-abiding citizens had very little chance to survive. People became indifferent to the local politics and lost confidence in each other; they could relax only in the company of their close and trusted friends. In short, the Darwin theory, the one of the "survival of the fittest", was put into practice for a thorough and comprehensive evaluation.

In such a situation not everybody followed the example of the gullible opera singer or windshield cleaners. The craftiest and shrewdest among us found other ways to ensure a solid start of their new lives. Some invested all their savings into precious stones, for example. Such a person would buy on the black market a diamond, with the size corresponding to the size of his capital and swallow it a couple hours prior to the body search by the custom officers at the border. And then, for the next several days, he would shit on the piece of paper and scrutinize his excrements in the search for the discharged treasure. Others found different, although similarly inconvenient, but still profitable venues.

When these "homo sovieticus" reached Italian shores their unconventional behavior shocked local landlords not less than Italian lifestyle shocked ill-informed immigrants.

The newly born Soviet "entrepreneurs", for example, in the last days of their "Roman holidays", were calling relatives in New York city and in Los Angeles and spending hours in lovely conversations regarding approaching rendezvous and future business plans and then the owners of the apartments paid the telephone company astronomical bills, sometimes up to several hundreds of dollars. The bills, obviously, were coming after the departure of the tenants. In order to combat this nasty pandemic of deceit the landlords, following the short period of confusion, canceled international services. They did not realize who they dealt with. The "builders of communism" were not the amateur mafia bosses. Now, instead of calling relatives in Brooklyn, the relatives from Brooklyn started to call newly arriving immigrants. Collect. And the bills from the telephone company had doubled.

The immigrants brought some changes even to the local infrastructure. Since their arrival the town of Ladispoli acquired two new rival organizations: Jewish synagogue and Baptist club. The majority of the immigrants consistently attended both. Not because they were practicing Jews or devoted Christians. On the contrary, they didn't give a damn about either religion. The reason for such an extraordinary turnout was simple: the Baptist club was offering them free cookies while the synagogue — free tea. So, first they were going to the club to watch the movie about Jesus Christ and his deeds and then to the synagogue, to find out that the guy was just a sorcerer and imposter. And have a great supper with the hot tea and chocolate cookies.

As once Karl Marx, the greatest socialist of all the socialists and whose expressions we had to learn by heart, said: "It is not the consciousness of men that determines their being, but on the contrary, their social being that determines their consciousness."

In the USA embassy in Rome we were asked to fill in the forms to substantiate our claims that we are not economical but political refugees. We needed to provide American authorities with the proof that back in the USSR we were objects of religious and/or ethnical persecution and corroborate it with the concrete examples of our mistreatment. However, in many cases the abuse was on such small scale and looked so pathetic in comparison to the Holocaust, that we found it to be ridiculous even to mention. And how, for example, a prisoner can convince a jury that he is still an oppressed person even if his jailer is a nice human and doesn't abuse him? Or is it possible for a leper to explain to a healthy individual what does it mean to be a leper? American laws were not formulated for us.

Fortunately, obtaining permission to immigrate to the United States was still among the easiest ones. Other countries, such as Canada, Australia and New Zealand as well as proof of political and religious persecution, had additional requirements, like maximum average family age, education, professional qualification and others.

I remember one joke from those turbulent times. A new immigrant arrives in Vienna and at the Jewish agency he is asked by the representative of that organization to which country he wishes to go? Is it Israel? "Of course not," he says, "there is a war there." "All right. How about the USA then?" "Oh, no," he says, "too much crime there." "Which country do you want to go to then?" "Could I see the world map?" the immigrant asked the clerk. And when the map was brought in and he thoroughly scrutinized it for at least half an hour, he turned back to the clerk and asked him one more question: "Do you, by any chance, have another map?"

Over the time, though, everyone settled in one or another country and started a new life.

For me it was hard at the beginning — I had to study and work simultaneously: the new language and the new customs, the new hardware and the new methods of using it, new sets of the laws and new relations among people — everything was new to me.

Everything I had to learn. For more than a year I was burning the candle at both ends. Or as one of our fellow immigrants correctly noticed: "during my first year in America I was spitting with my blood."

But eventually everything worked out

As to Lithuania — I haven't visited it yet. Not yet. Even after so many years of absence. I just didn't have time to do it. Besides, there are many other places which I want to see first.

However, if any of you decide to spend some time in the lush greenery of the farmlands and rolling hills, listen to the sedating murmur of the slow-moving rivers and inhale the intoxicating fragrance of the coniferous forests, I may assure you that you won't be sorry. Most likely the local guide will also show you many sights of the tremendous achievements of that small but talented nation: a formidable Trakai castle, the former residence of the Lithuanian kings, and an impressive Vilnius tower, looming over the medieval part of the city, narrow picturesque streets of the old towns and marvelous examples of the modern architecture. In the museum of fine art you will be introduced to the distinctive paintings of the idiosyncratic and unique Lithuanian artist Cherlionis, while the local artisans will offer you the elegant pieces of jewelry made from the natural amber, the one the Baltic Sea brings ashore during its violent storms. And someone will probably tell you the legend behind it, a love story between the sea princess Jurate and the fisherman Kastytis. Someone else maybe will narrate to you another delightful folk tale: this one about Egle, the queen of serpents. You will taste the famous Lithuanian beer — the centuries' old pride of the local brewers, and distinctive dishes of the Baltic cuisine. And very likely you will hear the profound lines from the poem of the famous Lithuanian poet Maironis, the lines which almost every Lithuanian knows by heart: "Where the river Sheshupe runs and flows the gracious Nemunas river — there is my beloved homeland, my beautiful Lithuania..."

But then someone may ask, "How about Jews? What did they leave behind after more than six hundred years of mutual coexistence? What impact did they make on the place they shared for so long?"

What they left behind are the gravestones at the sites of mass executions scattered all over the country. The guide will not show you them unless you specifically ask, but then, again, these gravestones are also part of the Lithuanian heritage. Just like the famous Gediminas tower.

Here is the one of the many mass graves, the resting place for over four hundred victims. It lays near the town of Babtai, several hundred feet off the old, presently unused road between the cities of Kaunas and Klaipeda, in a deserted and quiet spot on the left bank of the Nevezis river and the trees of the surrounding it forest are sheltering accidental passerby from the uncomfortable encounter.

The site has two gravestones.

The bottom one was put in during Soviet times. The epitaph doesn't mention that the victims of the massacre (buried behind the fence) were Jews; it only states that they were "peaceful Soviet citizens from the towns of Babtai and Vandziogala". This type of approach was customary in the Soviet Union. It came as the consequence of the communist doctrine which claimed that all people, disregarding their ethnicity and religion, are the same and equal. And since they all are equal then the Nazis effectively had to persecute them also equally, in the same exact way. For the Soviet Jews, however, this attitude of the government was an equivalent to the Holocaust denial.

The second gravestone, on the top of the first one, was put in when Lithuania became an independent state. It asserts that the victims were exclusively Jews.

Epilogue

One year has passed since I began to write my memoirs: a miniscule moment of time . A brief flash. Just like our own lives are. Just like the life of the Soviet Union, as a country, was on the scale of humanity. And I keep wondering what people will think about it in a thousand years from now? How will it be seen then from their perspective?

Now, since I have finished my project, I may ask myself something too: did I accomplish the task I planned to do? Did I answer the questions I planned to answer? Will my narrative make it easier for my daughter and her friends or for any curious fellow to understand what had happened in the Soviet Union? Will it help the future generations to avoid past mistakes?

I think it is up to the readers to make a judgement.

www.ingramcontent.com/pod-product-compliance
Lightning Source LLC
LaVergne TN
LVHW091544060526
838200LV00036B/693